More praise for *The Ten-Minute Inservice*

"Todd Whitaker and Annette Breaux offer concise, practical suggestions for reinforcing effective teaching practices. *The Ten-Minute Inservice* is a powerful resource for school leaders who want to make the most of every opportunity to promote growth and improve school climate."

—**Justin Baeder**, director, The Principal Center

"An integral piece of building teacher capacity is the transformation of faculty meetings, from a time for sitting and listening to an opportunity for reflecting and learning. Whitaker and Breaux demonstrate how simply that can be done with quick, easily implemented inservice activities that focus on the fundamentals of teaching."

—**John G. Gabriel**, principal, John Champe High School, Loudoun County, Virginia; coauthor, Dealing with the Tough Stuff

THE TEN-MINUTE INSERVICE

40 Quick Training Sessions that Build Teacher Effectiveness

Todd Whitaker
Annette Breaux

JOSSEY-BASS
A Wiley Imprint
www.josseybass.com

Cover illustration: ©Bienchen-s/Shutterstock

Cover design: Charles Brock, FaceOut Studio

Published by Jossey-Bass

A Wiley Imprint

One Montgomery Street, Suite 1200, San Francisco, CA 94104-4594—www.josseybass.com

Jossey-Bass books and products are available through most bookstores. To contact Jossey-Bass directly call our Customer Care Department within the U.S. at 800-956-7739, outside the U.S. at 317-572-3986, or fax 317-572-4002.

Wiley publishes in a variety of print and electronic formats and by print-on-demand. Some material included with standard print versions of this book may not be included in e-books or in print-on-demand. If this book refers to media such as a CD or DVD that is not included in the version you purchased, you may download this material at http://booksupport.wiley.com. For more information about Wiley products, visit www.wiley.com.

Library of Congress Cataloging-in-Publication Data
Whitaker, Todd, 1959-
  The ten-minute inservice : 40 quick training sessions that build teacher effectiveness / Todd Whitaker, Annette Breaux.
    pages cm
  Includes index.
  1. Effective teaching.   I. Breaux, Annette L.   II. Title.
  LB1025.3.W44 2013
  371.102—dc23   2012049784
ISBN 978-1-118-47043-5 (pbk.)
ISBN 978-1-118-55115-8 (ebk.)
ISBN 978-1-118-55116-5 (ebk.)
ISBN 978-1-118-55117-2 (ebk.)

Printed in the United States of America

FIRST EDITION

PB Printing   SKY10034939_062422

Contents

About the Authors

Dr. Todd Whitaker has been fortunate to be able to blend his passion with his career. He is recognized as a leading presenter in the field of education, and his message about the importance of teaching has resonated with hundreds of thousands of educators around the world. Todd is a professor of educational leadership at Indiana State University in Terre Haute, Indiana, and he has spent his life pursuing his love of education by researching and studying effective teachers and principals.

Prior to moving into higher education, Todd was a math teacher and basketball coach in Missouri. He then served as a principal at the middle school, junior high, and high school levels. He was also a middle school coordinator in charge of staffing, curriculum, and technology for the opening of new middle schools.

One of the nation's leading authorities on staff motivation, teacher leadership, and principal effectiveness, Todd has written thirty books, including the national best seller, *What Great Teachers Do Differently*. Other titles include *Shifting the Monkey, Dealing with Difficult Teachers, Teaching Matters, Great Quotes for Great Educators, What Great Principals Do Differently, Motivating and Inspiring Teachers,* and *Dealing with Difficult Parents.*

Todd is married to Beth, also a former teacher and principal, who is a professor of elementary education at Indiana State University. They are the parents of three children, Katherine, Madeline, and Harrison.

■ ■ ■

Annette Breaux is one of the most entertaining, informative authors and speakers in education. She leaves her audiences with practical techniques to implement in their schools and classrooms immediately. Administrators agree that they see results from teachers the next day.

Annette is a former classroom teacher, curriculum coordinator, and author of Louisiana FIRST, a statewide induction program for new teachers. Annette also served as the teacher induction coordinator for Nicholls State University in Thibodaux, Louisiana. She coauthored *New Teacher Induction* with Dr. Harry K. Wong.

Her other writings include *101 Answers for New Teachers and Their Mentors; REAL Teachers, REAL Challenges, REAL Solutions; 101 Poems for Teachers; Seven Simple Secrets: What the BEST Teachers Know and Do; 50 Ways to Improve Student Behavior;* and *Making Good Teaching Great.*

Teachers who have read Annette's writings or heard her speak agree that they come away with user-friendly information, heartfelt inspiration, and a reminder that theirs is the most noble of all professions.

How to Use This Book

If you're an administrator or a staff developer, your days are already crammed with meetings, projects, and crises. Still, you're charged with finding ways to maximize teacher effectiveness. So we've given you forty simple, easy-to-implement inservices designed to improve teaching and learning, each of which can be completed in ten minutes.

Even the book's design is deliberately simple, its format easy to follow. Each inservice is divided into three parts:

1. Purpose

2. Inservice

3. Implementation

In other words, the three sections will tell you what each inservice will accomplish, give you the content, and then show you exactly how to move from talk to action. There's no particular order to the inservices. Some do refer back to the previous inservice or build on its lesson. But each stands alone, and you can skip around as your teachers' needs require. There is no right or wrong way to use the book. Decide which inservices will work for you and when you'd like to use them. Each inservice will give you a quick, effective way to provide useful, meaningful, ongoing training for your teachers. And they've all been designed to take the least possible amount of time.

Because our focus was on inservices that can be conducted in a short amount of time, there are some topics that we have not been able to cover as they are too complex to tackle in a mini-workshop. These include differentiation, data analysis, and assessment, to name a few. However, the inservices provided here cover topics that are vital for good teaching, and implementing them with your staff should lead to schoolwide improvement.

Note: The Appendix includes a number of tips for making these inservices effective and engaging.

At the end of each inservice, we've left a section for notes. Use this section when you're preparing for the inservice, and use it again after you conduct the inservice, to add ideas and document results. These notes will prove invaluable the next time you conduct the inservice.

If you are a principal, you might choose to conduct all the inservices yourself. You might also choose to use a staff development trainer or one of your assistant administrators to conduct some of the inservices. If you have new teachers on staff, they will benefit from all the inservices, so you may choose to have one of your new-teacher mentors or your new-teacher induction coordinator use this book as an ongoing course. If your teachers meet regularly by grade level or subject area, this book can easily coordinate with those meetings. And it's a perfect fit for professional learning communities. Basically, this book will benefit any teacher, any administrator, and any staff development professional.

Think of it as quick, easy, meaningful, *doable* professional development.

Note that many of the inservices include material that can be displayed during your presentation or handed out to inservice participants. Those materials are available for free download from our publisher's website, at www.josseybass.com/go/10minuteinservice. Throughout the book, we'll remind you which materials can be downloaded by displaying the following icon:

Introduction

Do you want to see your students' achievement soar? Then improve the teaching in your school. It really is that simple.

How, though, do you improve teaching when you don't have time to grab a cup of coffee, let alone monitor every teacher's classes, hold private review sessions with them, and conduct weekly faculty meetings? It's not even practical to take up an entire faculty meeting with teaching demonstrations; everybody's too busy.

So we'll show you how to accomplish your goals with simple, clear-cut ten-minute inservices. Who says faculty meetings have to last an hour? **One of the most important goals of every faculty meeting should be for all teachers to walk out more excited about teaching and more effective tomorrow than they were today.** In this book, we'll show you how to conduct brisk, efficient ten-minute inservices that will improve teaching immediately. Teachers will look *forward* to these meetings. And you, the administrator or staff developer, will become a more effective instructional leader.

FACT: Better teaching leads to better student learning—and improved student outcomes.

1

As an administrator or staff developer, you want to ensure that all teachers are continually improving. **Basically, there are three types of teachers: ineffective teachers, good teachers, and great teachers**. You're responsible for helping all three groups improve their effectiveness. The ultimate goal, of course, is to have nothing but great teachers in your school. The day that that happens, you can relax and start your novel. But in the meantime, there are quick, specific steps you can take to make an immediate difference in the quality of teaching in every single classroom.

If you take an ineffective teacher and help that teacher become better, you have just improved student achievement in that teacher's classroom. That's not to say that this teacher is now a great teacher; chances are good that he isn't. We're also not suggesting that this teacher's students will outscore the students in better teachers' classrooms; that's not realistic. But the teacher will be better, and that is what we're focusing on—*improvement*. (If a teacher simply cannot improve, then he or she shouldn't be teaching, period.) If you take a good teacher and help that teacher improve, again, you have just improved student achievement in that teacher's classroom. And if you take a great teacher and help her improve, you have just ratcheted her students' achievements even higher. Now every student in your school has improved.

Great school leaders aren't aiming to make every teacher perfect. There's no such thing as a perfect teacher. Instead, great leaders continually strive to help each teacher—whether ineffective, good, or great—improve on a daily basis. *The Ten-Minute Inservice* **will show you how to improve both teaching and learning, in the fastest, easiest way possible.**

You'll be making yourself a great leader, ten minutes at a time!

PART 1

Classroom Management

Securing Students' Attention

PURPOSE

FACT 1: All effective teachers are effective classroom managers.

FACT 2: Even the most effective teachers work diligently to continually improve their classroom management skills.

FACT 3: Not all teachers are effective classroom managers.

FACT 4: Without effective management skills, effective teaching cannot occur.

FACT 5: *All* teachers possess the ability to become more effective, yet many fail to do so because they lack management skills. This leads us back to FACT 1: **All effective teachers are effective classroom managers**.

Any administrator will admit that if all teachers were effective classroom managers, discipline problems would be dramatically diminished, and learning would improve instantly.

Though we are not downplaying the importance of content knowledge, all the content knowledge in the world will not make someone an effective classroom manager. **You cannot teach any of the content effectively until you can manage the students**. Thus, in the classroom of a teacher who lacks effective management skills, effective teaching simply cannot occur.

Believe it or not, what many administrators and staff developers fear most about conducting an inservice is securing and keeping the attention of their audience. Have you ever attended an inservice and watched the presenter struggle—and fail—to get and keep everyone's attention? Or an inservice where attendees spoke out of turn? Or an inservice whose presenter, as a last resort, strained her voice to present *over* the talking of attendees? Those are not effective inservices. Likewise, have you ever observed a teacher struggling to get and keep his students' attention? That's not an effective lesson.

The good news is that there is a simple, effective solution. And that's the focus of today's inservice.

INSERVICE

Begin today's inservice by asking your teachers, *What is the most important procedure that any teacher must have?* Allow them a couple of minutes to share their answers. When they have finished, tell them that all of their answers are good and valid. However, the single most important procedure any teacher needs is a way of securing the students' attention.

Having established that fact, ask the next question: *What is your procedure for securing your students' attention? In other words, what is the one thing you do, consistently, every time you need the attention of your students?* Far too many teachers do not have one procedure solidly established for securing their students' attention. You know this already, of course, based on your ongoing observations of your teachers. Some say, "I need your attention." If saying this doesn't work the first time, they repeat it—often three or four times—until it does. If "I need your attention" still doesn't work, they try variations: "Excuse me. Stop the talking." Some resort to threats. And most of these teachers look unhappy while they're trying to get their students' attention. The list of methods is long, but the results are the same: chatty, distracted students.

Your best teachers, of course, will be happy to share some effective techniques for securing student attention. Though the sharing of ideas is important, keep in mind that this is a training session and that you are the trainer. You'll want to demonstrate an effective way of securing students' attention.

Here is ours. Feel free to use it:

Tell the students, "There will be times when I will need your undivided attention. When I need your attention, I will do two things. Here's what I will do." At this point, smile and raise your hand. Ask the students, "What two things do you see me doing?" (Note that they will almost always notice the smile first.) Once they have answered, say, "When you see me doing these two things, I need for you to stop talking and raise your hand. That will be your signal to me that I have your attention." Then say, "Now we will practice it. When I say 'Go,' start talking as much as you'd like. When I raise my hand and smile, stop talking and raise your hand. Go!" [Note that you will be demonstrating this for the teachers, so they will be the students for this activity.] *Allow the room to get noisy. Then smile and raise your hand, and do not begin speaking until all hands are raised and the room is quiet again. It will take only a few seconds, by the way.* [You will also notice that some of the teachers (students) will smile also, though this is not a condition of the procedure.] *Smiles are contagious. And smiling teachers experience far fewer power struggles with their students.*

Okay, so here you are, smiling and raising your hand. When everyone is quiet, say, "Thanks for following the procedure. But just so you know, students won't follow it that quickly. So you will simply continue to practice the procedure with your students. Remind them when they forget. Continue to implement the procedure consistently, with a smile on your face. The moment you appear upset, they win, you lose, and no procedure will work." [This will be addressed in detail in Inservice 6, "The Biggest Mistake Teachers Make."]

Remind your teachers that procedures apply to all grade levels. There's nothing "elementary" about them. Professional football coaches implement procedures and practice them over and over and over, every day. That's how their teams win.

Finally, remind your teachers that classroom management begins to go awry when teachers stop being consistent. The bottom line is that you have to have a way, one way, of reliably securing your students' attention. You have to use that procedure consistently. And if you do so with a pleasant look on your face, you remove the allure of a power struggle.

Tell your teachers that you will use this procedure with them for faculty meetings from here on out. It's also a great idea to implement a schoolwide procedure for student assemblies.

IMPLEMENTATION

You have demonstrated for your teachers a procedure for securing students' attention. Now you want them to go to their classrooms and implement this new procedure. If some teachers already have a procedure that works well for them, then tell them to continue it, by all means, and to share it with their colleagues. Your teachers don't have to use the exact procedure that you've shared. You simply want them to implement one consistent procedure for securing the attention of their students. It is important to note, however, that whatever procedure they implement should have two components: (1) it has to be consistently implemented, and (2) they have to look happy while they are implementing it.

Tell the teachers that you will be walking through classrooms this week (and in the future) observing their procedures for securing students' attention. When you meet a teacher in the hallway, especially one who struggles with classroom management, ask how the new procedure is working.

Once you have each teacher implementing a consistent procedure for securing student attention, discipline problems will improve immediately. And now that your teachers have a way of securing attention, they can move forward in establishing better overall classroom management. Stay on top of this one and continue to monitor its implementation. Teachers who are consistent have fewer students who are resistant!

Notes

_____
_____
_____
_____
_____
_____
_____
_____
_____
_____
_____
_____
_____
_____
_____
_____
_____
_____
_____
_____
_____
_____
_____
_____
_____
_____
_____
_____
_____
_____

Inservice 2

Establishing Rules and Procedures

PURPOSE

Have you ever noticed that your best teachers have the fewest discipline problems? Is it because you've given them the best-behaved students in the school? Probably not. Have you noticed that your best teachers almost always possess the happiest demeanors in the school? Who wouldn't be happy when their students are behaving so well? Yet you may have also noticed that these teachers have the fewest rules of anyone in the school. Have you noticed that the few rules they do have are enforced consistently?

Your best teachers will tell you that they rarely have to discipline a student for breaking a rule. Yet those same students are breaking rules left and right in the classrooms of other teachers. So what are the secrets known only to the very best teachers? Not only will we share these secrets, but we'll guarantee that anyone who implements them will begin to experience fewer discipline problems.

Speaking of problems, let's establish just what the main problem is when teachers are struggling to manage their classrooms. If you walk through almost any school, you will notice that most teachers post their rules somewhere on a classroom wall. Notice that there is often a rule to "raise your hand before speaking." It can be stated in many ways, but the point is that this particular "rule" has something to do with talking. This is a giant red flag: it alerts you that these teachers do not understand the difference between rules and procedures. And because the most basic components of classroom management are rules and procedures, good classroom management will be lacking in these classrooms.

Regrettably, many teachers do not possess a basic understanding of classroom management because they've never been taught the difference between rules and procedures.

Today you will teach them.

And, by the way, knowing the difference between rules and procedures and implementing them consistently is the first secret to the success of your very best teachers. Another secret is that they have very few rules and lots of procedures. By the end of today's ten-minute inservice, all your teachers will know what the best teachers have already figured out.

INSERVICE

After greeting each teacher today as he or she enters the faculty meeting, use the procedure you established in Inservice 1, "Securing Students' Attention." Spend a minute or two allowing a few to share how their new procedures for securing student attention have been working. Remind them that consistently implementing such a procedure was necessary to get them to the next step of classroom management.

Tell your teachers that today you will be sharing some of the secrets of effective classroom managers. These secrets will help them have fewer discipline problems. Share the fact that many teachers, through no fault of their own, do not understand the difference between a rule and a procedure. And because clearly established rules and procedures are the key to effective classroom management, a lack of understanding of the difference between the two can lead to many discipline problems.

Provide the following example to prove your point:

Some teachers have a rule about talking. Yet talking is not a serious offense. An aggravating offense? Yes. A serious offense? No. Because rules regulate serious offenses only, then talking out of turn falls under the category of "procedure" as opposed to "rule."

Make and share a copy of the following for each teacher:

Rules and Procedures Simplified

- A rule regulates a serious offense.
- A procedure is simply a way that you want something done in your classroom—the same way, every time.
- When a student breaks a rule, a consequence follows.
- When a student does not follow a procedure, you remind him of the procedure and practice it with him if necessary.
- You should never have more than five rules.
- You should have many procedures.
- An example of a rule: *We agree not to hit each other.* (Fighting is a serious offense.)
- Examples of procedures include *how to walk to lunch, how to ask permission to speak, how to get into and out of groups, what to do if you need a pencil sharpened,* and *how to pass in papers.*

You will probably notice that once teachers are clear about the difference between rules and procedures, most will have trouble thinking of five rules. Some have only one or two. This is fine, as long as those one or two are enforced consistently.

Make the point that all effective classroom managers have lots of procedures. However, they do not implement them all at once. Rather, they implement the most important ones first (such as a procedure for securing the attention of their students), and they continue to add a few at a time. In the classrooms of effective managers, students are never confused about what is expected of them. The procedures are discussed, modeled, and practiced. When a student forgets, he is reminded of the correct procedure. If practice is needed, it is provided by the teacher. If a rule is broken, there is no discussion; rather, there is a consequence. The students know this, so there is no element of surprise. They do much less "testing of the teacher" to see how much they can get away with. Structured, preestablished rules and procedures, followed consistently, equal a well-managed classroom every time.

Please note (and share with your teachers) that chronic misbehavior can lead to consequences for one or two particular students. For instance, if a teacher has a procedure for talking out of turn, and one student continues to talk out of turn after much practice and many reminders, then the teacher might need to inform the student that the next time he talks out of turn, there will be a consequence. Teachers should be very cautious about this, of course. Doling out a consequence for violating a procedure should be used only when the misbehavior is chronic, not simply because the teacher is aggravated. As we stated, rules are used to regulate serious offenses. Although talking out of turn is not a serious offense, it can lead to consequences if and when the behavior becomes a chronic problem. In Inservice 3, "Effective Ways to Address Misbehavior," we will share a strategy that works beautifully when dealing with chronic talkers.

IMPLEMENTATION

Knowing the secrets to successful classroom management is not enough—you have to be able and willing to implement them. So now, send your teachers off with a two-part assignment: (1) have each decide on no more than five rules and introduce those rules to the students; (2) have each determine their procedures and begin implementing and practicing them. Note that in Inservice 3, "Effective Ways to Address Misbehavior," we will provide a strategy for dealing with a student who does not follow a particular procedure. Today's goal is to ensure that all teachers are clear on the difference between rules and procedures so that they can begin implementing both on a consistent basis.

When students are clear on exactly what they can and cannot do in the classroom, and when they know that the teacher is consistent in enforcing rules and practicing procedures, they are much more likely to actually follow the rules and procedures. Ask any effective classroom manager!

Notes

Inservice 3

Effective Ways to Address Misbehavior

PURPOSE

When a student does something inappropriate in class, he is usually expecting the teacher to react in a certain way. He knows he has an audience (his classmates), and he is often putting on a performance. Many teachers make the mistake of dealing with this type of student in front of his audience, and the behavior rarely improves. In fact, a bad situation usually worsens. Great teachers, of course, have effective ways of dealing with this type of student. They talk one-on-one, in private, defusing any hope of a power struggle or an Oscar-winning performance on the part of the student.

In Inservice 2, "Establishing Rules and Procedures," you taught all of your teachers the difference between rules and procedures, and you sent them off to establish their own. Undoubtedly, your weakest teachers are complaining that some students just won't follow the procedures. Remember, you gave them the worst students in the school! But, in their defense, most of these teachers are doing the best they can with the skills they possess. They have not yet fully grasped the concept of classroom management, and they still lack a full bag of tricks. They continue to engage in power struggles with students, forgetting that they are the adults in the classroom. They still don't understand how important it is to be consistent in enforcing rules and implementing procedures.

The good news is that through these inservice sessions, you are helping stock their bags with useful strategies for dealing with student misbehavior. Regarding those teachers who are already effective classroom managers, please don't ever feel that you will be boring them with unnecessary inservice sessions. On the contrary, your very best teachers are always looking to add to their own bag of tricks. They are also silently high-fiving you for helping the less effective teachers change their ways.

Today we will share one of our favorite ways to break a student (of any age) of an inappropriate behavior.

INSERVICE

After greeting your teachers as they enter the inservice and using your procedure for getting their attention, say:

In previous inservices, we have discussed ways to secure students' attention and to establish clear rules and procedures with them. Have you had any students who occasionally still don't follow all of your procedures? Do you have students who are chronic talkers and are failing to raise their hands and ask for permission to speak?

By the way, even your best teachers occasionally experience such situations. So you will have the rapt attention of all your teachers. Tell them that today you will be sharing an effective technique for dealing with a student who is behaving inappropriately or is regularly ignoring one of your procedures. (Note that we are not talking about a student who fails to follow a procedure once or twice.)

Here's the technique: THE PRIVATE PRACTICE SESSION

(Note that although you will be dealing with a chronic talker in this example, the technique can be used with any misbehavior.)

When a student is chronically talking out of turn, meet with the student privately and say, in a tone of concern and not frustration, "I've noticed that you're having trouble remembering our procedure for raising your hand before speaking.

Don't be too hard on yourself for forgetting. I'm an adult, and I often forget things. But I know how embarrassing it can be to forget so often in front of your friends. So here's what I'm willing to do for you. I will give you my recess today and practice with you so that you will become really good at following that procedure and be less likely to forget. I'm happy to do that for you. See you at recess." That's it. In essence, you are pretending that you think that the student is just forgetting to raise his hand. Surely he would not be purposely ignoring the procedure! The key is that you are not at all sarcastic and that you tell the student you are willing to give of your own time to help him. Do you see what you just did? You did not take his recess from him, but rather you gave him yours!

So the student comes in at recess, and you say, "Thanks for coming in. Okay, now pretend that we are in class and you have something you want to say. Show me what you'll do." The student slowly raises his hand and you say, "Great! I can give you fifteen more minutes of practice. Do you think you need more practice, or do you feel you have it now?" The student always says, "I have it." Then say, "Great. See you tomorrow. Oh, if you forget again tomorrow, that's my fault. That simply means I didn't give you enough practice. I'll even stay after school for you if you need. Just let me know."

Please note that this technique takes less than a minute, so the good news is that you do not lose your own recess after all. And if you teach in a school where there is no recess, you can use this technique between classes, during your planning period, during class while the other students are working independently, during lunch, and so on.

One final note: some teachers may ask, "Well, what if the student does not show up at recess?" The answer is simple: *Go and find him and say, "Oh, you must have forgotten that you and I have a practice session. Let's go." And you do this with a smile on your face.*

IMPLEMENTATION

This week's assignment is for all teachers to use the private practice session at least once with a student. Chances are good that they will have more than one opportunity to try the new technique. But you're only asking for each to try it at least once. If they implement it appropriately, they'll be using it from here on out.

End the session by saying, *The private practice session strategy is a simple one that produces amazing results. Anyone who tells you that private practice sessions with students don't work has obviously never tried them or is not using them appropriately. Practice makes perfect, doesn't it? So practice your private practice sessions and you'll soon see fewer behavior indiscretions.*

Notes

_____

_____

_____

_____

_____

_____

_____

_____

_____

_____

_____

_____

_____

_____

_____

_____

_____

_____

_____

_____

_____

_____

_____

_____

This inservice is adapted from Annette Breaux and Todd Whitaker, *50 Ways to Improve Student Behavior* (Larchmont, NY: Eye on Education, 2010), pp. 51, 52. www.eyeoneducation.com

Sharing Classroom Management Tips

PURPOSE

You have spent the previous three inservices providing simple, useful, easy-to-implement techniques for improving classroom management. However, no teacher ever finishes learning to manage a classroom. Your best teachers are always hungry for new tips, tricks, and strategies, and your less-than-best teachers desperately need them. Today your teachers will receive yet more tips, techniques, and strategies for improving classroom management. But this time, they will be learning from each other.

INSERVICE

Begin today's inservice by sharing the following poem:

How Does One Manage a Classroom?

"How does one manage a classroom? Is it really rocket science?
For I've been told that it's difficult to control so much student defiance."
Well, management is about the teacher, and what the teacher expects
Because everything about the teacher absolutely affects
How students will or won't respond, how they will or will not act,
And with excellent classroom management, students behave well. That's a
  fact!
So set clear rules and procedures, and show how you want things done
And remember that on the scale of importance, being consistent is number
  one!
Consistent in how you treat each one, consistent in your preparation,
Consistent in being professional, regardless of your level of frustration,
Consistent in saying what you mean and meaning what you say,
Consistent in making every student feel special every day,
Consistent in your refusal to give up on anyone,
Consistent in helping students to see a task through 'til it's done,
Consistent in having a good attitude, for your attitude sets the tone,
Consistent in being available, so that no student feels alone,
Consistent in helping every child to know he can succeed,
Yes, being consistent is the key to classroom management, indeed!
Being consistent is not difficult---just be consistent at being consistent---
And soon your discipline problems will be a memory that is distant!

This poem is from Annette Breaux, *101 Answers for New Teachers and Their Mentors*, 2nd ed. (Larchmont, NY: Eye on Education, 2011), p. 1. www.eyeoneducation.com

After sharing the poem, say, *I see many wonderful management techniques working well in lots of our classrooms. So today I'm going to ask you to share some of your own management tips with each other. Take a minute or two to think of a management strategy that works particularly well for you. Then I'll ask some of you to share those strategies.*

Next, spend a few minutes allowing teachers to share their successes with one another. Because this is a ten-minute inservice, you will not have time for everyone to share, and that's okay. You simply want to get them thinking and talking. When you call on teachers to share their ideas, don't just call on your star teachers. But *do* call on a few of them. Also, it's a good idea to have one of your less than effective classroom managers write the ideas on chart paper as they are shared. You want these teachers actively involved in these types of activities.

One principal shared the following experience with us:

> I conducted a ten-minute inservice where I had each teacher come up with one management strategy to share with the faculty. My most effective teachers were eager to share. The others were not so exuberant. I knew that would be the case, of course, before I gave the assignment. But I wanted to get everyone thinking about the importance of good classroom management. And it's a good idea to make your struggling teachers feel a little uncomfortable from time to time. First, they need to realize that what they are doing is ineffective, and second, they need to know that there are strategies that actually work. I won't allow them to blame their lack of success on the students.
>
> When it came time to share the strategies, I made it a point to call on some of my best teachers, some of my mediocre teachers, and some of my most ineffective teachers. I didn't ask for volunteers. I simply called on people to share. Then, when we ran out of time, I gave them each the task of writing about one of their most effective management strategies. We then compiled these and shared a copy with everyone. I had every teacher pick one new strategy from the compiled list to try in their own classrooms.
>
> This ten-minute inservice brought amazing results. My best teachers were thrilled with all the new ideas. The mediocre teachers were more than willing to attempt some new strategies. And the least effective teachers were left with no more excuses. A few of the teachers asked to see the techniques in action in other teachers' classrooms. I was more than happy to make that happen.

IMPLEMENTATION

The assignment this week is to send all your teachers off to write about one classroom management strategy that works well in their own classrooms. Remind them to keep their explanations to a few sentences. Set a quick deadline, ideally within a few days. Ask a volunteer to combine all ideas into one document, then provide each teacher with a copy. This is an excellent way to quickly add to everyone's bag of tricks!

As an added benefit, this provides you, the administrator or staff developer, with a nonthreatening reason to observe particular teachers who may need some extra guidance. For instance, you might say to Ms. LIM (Lacking in Management), "I liked the classroom management strategy you mentioned in the group document. I look forward to coming in and seeing it in action, because I'd love to find out more about it. Thanks."

Notes

_____

_____

_____

_____

_____

_____

_____

_____

_____

_____

_____

_____

_____

_____

_____

_____

_____

A Scream to Blow Off Steam

PURPOSE

I know just why you scream at me
You scream to blow off steam at me
And when your steam blows, everyone knows
You're as out of control as you seem to be!

Does this poem ring true for some of your teachers? We have yet to find a school without a few resident screamers—those teachers who can be heard loudly losing control of their own emotions when dealing with students. Why do they allow themselves to do this? Believe it or not, they're making a desperate attempt to regain the control they have handed over to the students. Think about the fact that they scream—which demonstrates a loss of control—in an attempt to gain control. Losing control in order to gain control has never worked and never will. But your screamers have not figured this out. Just as a camel cannot see its own hump, your screamers cannot see that the louder they become, the more out of control their students become.

If you were to walk into any school, anywhere, and ask the students, "Who are the screamers on the faculty?" could the students tell you? Of course they could, with 100 percent accuracy. In all schools, all students know all the screamers. And all the students dread being in the classrooms of these teachers. In fact, you often get calls from parents requesting that their children not be placed in So-and-So's classroom, don't you? We all know who these people are, and we often struggle with how to keep them under control. Well, one of the best ways to keep them under control is to take away their option of screaming at students.

You might be thinking right about now, "This inservice is only for a few teachers." We hope that's correct. But you will want all of your teachers witnessing the next ten minutes, because what you are about to do will help cement your status as a true leader in this school. True leaders insist on professionalism from *all* teachers, not most. And one of the most unprofessional behaviors of teachers is that of raising their voices in anger.

From today forward, however, everyone on your faculty will know the following: *When you raise your voice in anger with students, you publicly admit that you can't even control your own emotions. When you are not in control of your own emotions, you cannot possibly be in control of anyone else! And because we, as teachers, must be in control of our students at all times, it is simply not an option to raise our voices in anger. Period.*

INSERVICE

Begin by asking the following questions and allowing for brief discussion:

- Who are the professionals in this school? (We are.)
- As professionals, do we have a duty to serve as positive role models for our students? (Yes.)

- Is it ever okay to serve as negative role models for our students? (No.)

- But don't we get frustrated with students from time to time? (Yes.) And when we do, isn't it tempting to air those frustrations in front of our students? (Tempting, yes. But we just can't do it.)

- Have you ever been angry and frustrated, and tempted to raise your voice to a student? (Of course.) But if you give in to that, what message are you sending to that student and to anyone within earshot?

Tell your teachers, *The bottom line is that if you ever raise your voice to a student, the message is, "I have lost control of my own emotions. I have allowed you, a student, to control my emotions." And now the student knows that he can control you, so he will continue to control you all year long. The second and possibly more damaging message is that when you get really aggravated with someone, it is okay to lose your temper. That, of course, is the* last *message we ever want to give to our students. Therefore, it is never okay for any of us to scream at students.*

I've been approached with the idea of implementing a "No Screaming" policy, and I love the idea. So from today forward, we will implement such a policy. In other words, we will all agree that no matter how frustrated we may become, we will handle ourselves as professionals. Don't misunderstand: we will still hold students accountable. We just won't raise our voices when holding them accountable. Instead, we will hold them accountable in a rational and professional manner. If a student loses control of his emotions in your presence, make sure that only one person is out of control. In fact, the more out of control a student becomes, the calmer and more "in control" we must appear, if we have any hope of helping him regain control of his emotions. Shouting back at someone who is shouting at you does not make that person want to do anything but shout louder. But if he's shouting alone, it takes all the fun and fire out of it.

IMPLEMENTATION

When you send your teachers off to implement the new No Screaming policy, we recommend that you have them share this policy with the students. Let everyone in the school know that from here on out, adults will not scream at students in this school. You *will* hold students accountable, however, as you always have. By letting the students know of this new policy, you accomplish two things: (1) you help put the students at ease by providing them with a calmer, safer, more nonthreatening environment; (2) you add yet another measure of accountability for teachers who might be tempted to continue to scream at students when they think no adult will hear them. If teachers tell students that they won't be screaming anymore, the students will hold them to that promise.

Notes

_____
_____
_____
_____
_____
_____
_____
_____
_____
_____
_____
_____
_____
_____
_____
_____
_____
_____
_____
_____
_____

The Biggest Mistake Teachers Make

PURPOSE

The absolutely biggest mistake that teachers consistently make is this: they let students know that the students have gotten to them emotionally, have pushed their buttons. Here are some examples of what this mistake looks like in the classroom:

- Teacher raising his or her voice to a student in anger.

- Teacher speaking with clenched teeth.

- Teacher's face reddening, veins in the neck protruding.

- Teacher staring at the ceiling with arms folded. Possibly tapping foot.

- Teacher using the oh-so-dreaded stare, better known as "the Teacher Eye."

- Teacher saying, "I've had enough! Go to the office!"

We could go on, but you get the point. And surely you have seen all these behaviors, and then some, displayed by teachers in your own school. So what's the big deal? Students are aggravating at times. They try our patience, and yes, they push our buttons—BINGO! Students should never even know that their teachers *have* buttons.

INSERVICE

Begin the inservice by asking the following questions:

- How many of you have ever felt aggravated with a student?
- Have you ever been guilty of "taking the bait" with a student?
- Have you ever allowed your students to know that they have upset you on an emotional level? (We all have, at one time or another.)
- What happens when a student knows she has succeeded in pushing your buttons?

Following this brief discussion, make these points:

- The biggest mistake that we, as teachers, consistently make is this: we let students know that they have gotten to us emotionally. We show our frustration, and the students know they've won. They are now controlling our emotions.
- Understand that it is okay to let students know that you are disappointed by their actions. But there's a big difference between being disappointed in someone's actions and being personally offended by those actions.
- Also understand that it is definitely okay to hold students accountable for their actions. The key is to always hold students accountable in a professional, not emotional, manner. (We've already begun taking this step with our No Screaming policy.)

Next, ask teachers to come up with a few ways they could deal with student misbehavior calmly and professionally as opposed to emotionally. You may want to provide a few examples:

Example: A student is repeatedly making noises. You have asked him to stop, but the behavior has continued. How could you handle this effectively?

Example: Your students are working on an independent assignment at their seats. One student is not doing any work. How could you handle this effectively?

Example: Two students are laughing with one another. Other students are noticing, and the behavior has become distracting. How could you handle this effectively?

Example: A student walks into your classroom visibly upset about something that happened outside your classroom. You can see that the situation could be volatile. How could you handle this effectively?

Example: A student is upset with you and she lashes out, saying hurtful things to you. Your feelings are hurt, and you are embarrassed by her actions. How could you handle this effectively?

Add your own examples here if you choose:

_____

_____

_____

_____

_____

_____

_____

_____

_____

_____

IMPLEMENTATION

Tell your teachers, *We have just discussed several ways to deal with common misbehaviors in a calm and professional manner. This week, I'll ask each of you to document two ways you have dealt with student misbehavior without letting the student know that he or she has upset you. At the next inservice, I'll ask several of you to share those examples with the rest of us. If, due to time constraints in the next inservice, you don't get a chance to share yours, I'll keep everyone's documentation for possible sharing at a future inservice. Thanks.*

By asking them all to document their actions, you hold each teacher accountable for at least thinking about dealing with student misbehavior in a more professional manner. That's what you want. Get teachers thinking that way, and chances are better that they'll eventually act that way.

Note: You may or may not be conducting these inservices in the order that this book is written. Regardless of which inservice you choose to conduct next, don't forget to have at least a few teachers share their assignments from this inservice at the next inservice.

Notes

_____

_____

_____

_____

_____

_____

_____

_____

_____

_____

_____

_____

_____

_____

Learn to Ignore More

PURPOSE

Have you ever gone on a long car trip with young children? After only ten minutes, did one of them ask, "How much farther is it?" When faced with this question, you, as an adult, are under no legal obligation to respond. In case you haven't figured this out yet, if you respond, the child will likely continue to ask the same question over and over and over. Finally, you might reach your limit and answer in an angry tone, daring him to ask the question again. However, if you extend your "ignoring zone," the frequency of the question is likely to diminish.

Have you ever witnessed an adult, be it a parent or teacher, playing yes-no Ping-Pong with a child? "I'm not going to do it!" "Yes you will." "No I won't." "Yes you will!" No one wins at this game. So the simple answer is not to play. Do not engage in power struggles with children. Simple? Yes. Easy? No.

The fact is that some behaviors are dealt with most effectively when they are ignored. But many teachers do not realize that this possibility even exists. They think they have to address every little situation every time. This leads to aggravation, frustration, and wasted teaching time. These teachers are constantly running around trying to put out fires and sometimes actually fueling the very fires they are attempting to extinguish. The act of ignoring in the classroom should not be confused with avoiding. Ignoring is an intentional action whereby the teacher chooses whether or not to respond to a student's behavior and if so, when. The choice to ignore is a strategy whereby the teacher is actually dealing with the situation by ignoring it in an attempt to diminish or stop a certain behavior. The strategy of ignoring is used often by effective teachers. Today you'll show all your teachers how to use this strategy effectively.

INSERVICE

Begin the inservice by sharing the "child on a long car trip" scenario. Ask if they've ever been guilty of playing yes-no Ping-Pong with a student in their classrooms. Explain to your teachers that sometimes it is more effective to ignore a student's behavior than to add any energy to the situation. The operative word here is "sometimes." There are many behaviors that cannot and should not be ignored.

Provide the following two scenarios and ask which of the two could be ignored and which could not be ignored:

Scenario 1: A student is upset because she does not like what you have just assigned. Everyone else gets busy, but she continues to try to let you see that she is sitting there, steaming, not getting busy.

Scenario 2: A student is cheating on a test. He is trying to be subtle, but the action is quite obvious to you.

Discuss the fact that scenario 1 could be ignored, in hopes that the student will eventually give up on trying to express her dissatisfaction with the assignment and get busy. Scenario 2 is a situation that cannot be ignored, for obvious reasons. So now you've established that there are some actions that can be ignored and some that cannot.

Next, give a few examples of typical classroom situations that could be ignored or possibly ignored temporarily until the teacher decides how and when to deal with them. After you discuss the following, have teachers add and discuss several situations of their own:

- A student tapping a pencil on his desk
- Two students whispering to one another
- A student with her head down on the desk
- A student who may be chewing gum, but so discreetly that you're not positive that he is
- A student making unusual noises in an attempt to gain attention
- A student passing a note to another student
- A student who is tattling about something insignificant
- A student who slams his books down as he gets to his desk in an attempt to let you know that he is upset about something
- A student using inappropriate language—and you overhear it
- _____
- _____
- _____
- _____
- _____

Now give a few examples of situations that should not be ignored. After discussing the following, have the teachers add and discuss several situations of their own:

- A student who is chronically tardy for class
- A student who is hurting another student
- A student who is threatening another student
- A student who is chronically sleeping in class

- A student whose behavior is causing such a disturbance that the other students cannot concentrate on their work

- _____

- _____

- _____

- _____

- _____

And now discuss the following benefits of ignoring (or temporarily ignoring) certain student behaviors. Allow your teachers to add a few benefits of their own.

- This gives you, the teacher, a chance to calm down.
- It guarantees that you will not add fuel to a burning fire.
- It allows you time to think and decide what to do, if anything, while continuing with class.
- It gives you the opportunity to deal with students individually, after class or away from the other students, taking away their coveted audience.

- _____

- _____

- _____

- _____

- _____

IMPLEMENTATION

Ask your teachers to practice their "ignoring" skills this coming week. Put a list titled "Ignore More" in the lounge or near the teachers' mailboxes or somewhere that is easily accessible to all. Tell them you would like each of them to add one example of a situation where using the strategy of ignoring has been beneficial in their classrooms. Once the list is complete, share it with everyone.

Pretending NOT to see
Can sometimes be
A very successful strategy.

Notes

_____
_____
_____
_____
_____
_____
_____
_____
_____
_____
_____
_____
_____
_____
_____
_____
_____
_____
_____

Simple Ways to Defuse Anger

PURPOSE

Will We Ever Learn?

I am angry and I'm going to let you know it
I'll make you angry too, and then you'll show it
And soon we'll fuel each other's flame
Neither will agree about who deserves the blame
But argue we will, and ridiculous we'll appear
To anyone who's able to overhear
Two shouting people who have both lost control
Repelling like magnets of a similar pole
It's ironic, but no one can win this game
Will we ever learn? If not, what a shame!

Have you ever been confronted by an angry parent? An angry teacher? An angry student? It's so tempting to be the people represented in the poem. Our survival instinct makes us want to engage and fuel each other's rage. For professionals, however, engaging is not an option. But haven't some of your teachers missed that memo? Acting calm in the face of an upheaval requires skill, and possessing this skill is a must for anyone who dares to call herself a teacher. Mastering this skill, however, requires lots of patience and lots of practice. What better time than now to teach your teachers how to master the art of remaining in control, regardless of how out of control someone else becomes.

Remember that most, if not all, of your teachers are doing the best they can with the skills they currently possess. They'd handle conflict much differently and more effectively if they only knew how. It is very likely that some of your teachers have never been taught how to handle conflict calmly, professionally, and effectively. Today you'll show them how.

INSERVICE

Begin by asking your teachers to consider the following points. You may want to have these points posted for everyone to see.

Points to Ponder

- If a flame is not fueled, it will soon burn out.
- When a person loses his cool, losing your cool in return will fuel his flame.
- When a person loses his cool, *not* losing your cool will cause his flame to eventually burn out.
- It is human nature to want to scream back at someone who is screaming at you.
- While on the job, it is unprofessional to scream at someone who is screaming at you.
- Two screaming people never solve any problems.
- As educators, you are sometimes confronted by parents or students who have lost their composure. When this happens, they are often looking to you to fuel their flame.
- It is never productive or appropriate for you, a professional, to lose control, no matter how out of control a parent or student becomes.
- If you're going to deal with an out-of-control person effectively, you have to defuse her anger before you can effectively address the cause of that anger.

Now ask, *Do any of you disagree with any of the points I've just made?* They won't disagree, because there is actually no logical argument to counteract any of these points. And when you have people agreeing with you, they're much more receptive to the idea of learning from you. At this point, you might choose to read the poem "Will We Ever Learn?" to them.

Next, provide a few examples of teachers dealing with angry parents and students. Let the teachers decide which of these are effective and which are ineffective.

Example 1: A student is refusing to do her work. The teacher warns her to get busy, and she screams, "I'm not doing it, and you can't make me!" The teacher responds by saying, "Yes I can. You'll do your work or else!" The student retorts, "Or else what?" The teacher says, "Or else you'll go to the office." The student says, "Good, send me to the office!"

Example 2: A student is refusing to do her work. The teacher calmly walks up to her and whispers, "Are you feeling okay? Do you need some help getting started? You look like you're not yourself today. Let me know if I can do anything to help."

It's obvious that example 2 is the more effective technique. The teacher remains calm. Instead of appearing frustrated because the student is not doing her work, the teacher acts out of concern. The teacher immediately removes the allure of a power struggle. Even if the student does not immediately get busy, the fact that there is no power struggle makes this approach infinitely more effective than example 1, where there is nothing but a power struggle. Teachers who approach students as the teacher does in example 2, however, rarely have problems getting off-task students back on task.

Example 3: An angry parent confronts a teacher. The parent screams, "I'm tired of the way you're treating Harrison! You punished him for something he did not do. You accused him of saying hurtful things to Maria. But she was the one who said hurtful things to him. You're always blaming him because you've got it out for him! I'm sick of this!" The teacher raises her voice in anger and says, "Yes he *did* say hurtful things to Maria. I've got witnesses who can attest to that because he did it in front of the rest of the class. You know what his problem is? You believe everything he tells you. I do *not* have it out for him. He deserved to be punished!"

Example 4: An angry parent confronts a teacher. The parent screams, "I'm tired of the way you're treating Harrison! You punished him for something he did not do. You accused him of saying hurtful things to Maria. But she was the one who said hurtful things to him. You're always blaming him because you've got it out for him! I'm sick of this!" The teacher calmly says, "Ms. Smith, I'd like to pay you a compliment. I don't know if you and I will leave each other agreeing or disagreeing today about what Harrison did, but the very fact that you cared enough to come to school and discuss this with me says to me that you are a concerned parent, and I respect that."

In which of these two examples do you think the parent will be more likely to work cooperatively with the teacher? There's no rocket science here. Dealing with anyone in a calm, professional manner increases the chances a hundredfold that the two of you can work together to solve a problem. Lashing out at someone guarantees the opposite result.

IMPLEMENTATION

Have each teacher choose a partner. If there is an uneven number, put three people together. Give them the following scenarios:

- A student walks into your classroom angry, saying, "You'd better tell Brandon to stop picking on me, or else I'll beat him up!" Describe how an ineffective teacher might handle this. Describe how an effective teacher might handle this.

- A student is visibly frustrated while taking her test. She tears the paper in two and says, "I'm not doing this. This is stupid!" Describe how an ineffective teacher might handle this. An effective teacher?

- A student begins arguing with another student in your classroom. The argument quickly escalates, and both are screaming at each other. The ineffective teacher's response? An effective teacher's response?

- A parent comes to you and accuses you of bullying his child by picking on him, not allowing him to sit next to his friends, and keeping him in at recess. It is true that you have changed where the child now sits in class, with good reason. It is true that you have kept the child in at recess to help him finish work he did not finish during class. Describe how an ineffective teacher might handle this conversation. An effective teacher?

Feel free to add your own examples, possibly addressing problems that your teachers are currently facing in their classrooms. Tell the teachers that they have one week to sit together and come up with effective and ineffective solutions to the sample problems you have just provided. At the end of the week, you might choose to have them come back together as a group to share their answers. Or you might choose to have a volunteer teacher compile all the answers into one document. Again, you're adding to their bags of tricks. You're allowing them to collaborate and learn from one another. You're also helping them reconsider their current methods of dealing with angry students or parents. It's a win-win all around.

Notes

PART 2

Teaching Practices

Effective Teaching, Part 1

PURPOSE

Effective teaching . . . what is it? Although it's difficult to define, it's easy to recognize. Students can recognize it, parents can recognize it, and, believe it or not, even ineffective teachers can recognize it when they see it in action. But being able to recognize something doesn't mean you know how to put it into action yourself.

Although ineffective teachers can recognize effective teaching when they see it, they are usually not capable of understanding all that goes into making the teaching they witness effective. At some level, they know that they are lacking in effectiveness. However, they are usually not aware of exactly what they are doing that is hampering their effectiveness. If they were aware, they would stop doing it; no one strives to be ineffective.

The purpose of today's inservice is to help your teachers—all of them—better understand the characteristics of both effective and ineffective teaching. This understanding is critical if we want to figure out what separates the best from all the rest.

INSERVICE

Tell your teachers that they will be taking a group test today. You are simply going to read a list of characteristics of teaching. For each item you read, if it is a characteristic of effective teaching, they are to raise their hands. If the characteristic is one of ineffective teaching, they are to put their heads down.

Effective Versus Ineffective Teaching Test

1. Begin lessons by saying, "Open your books to page ___." (ineffective)
2. Use lots of hands-on learning activities. (effective)
3. Enjoy a positive, friendly rapport with students. (effective)
4. Rely heavily on textbooks. (ineffective)
5. View and use textbooks as resources and teaching tools. (effective)
6. Smile often. (effective)
7. Appear serious most of the time. (ineffective)
8. Use lots of worksheets. (ineffective)
9. Raise your voice in anger and frustration when dealing with students. (ineffective)
10. Appear calm and professional at all times. (effective)
11. Allow for lots of structured student discussion during the learning process. (effective)
12. Often allow students to work together to solve problems. (effective)
13. Test what is taught in the same way that it has been taught. (effective)
14. Include "surprise" items on tests—items students did not know would be on the test. (ineffective)
15. Engage in power struggles with students when required. (ineffective)
16. Deal with student misbehavior in a private manner. (effective)
17. Embarrass students in front of their peers (ineffective)
18. Plan detailed lessons designed to maximize critical thinking, learning, and engagement. (effective)
19. Use the same lesson plans from year to year. (ineffective)

20. Constantly seek to learn new and better ways to teach. (effective)

21. Relate lessons to the lives of the students. (effective)

22. Resist change. (ineffective)

23. Accept and welcome change as a necessary part of growth. (effective)

24. Often speak of students with fondness. (effective)

25. Often speak of students with disapproval. (ineffective)

26. Express belief in each student. (effective)

27. Make tireless efforts to keep parents informed of student progress. (effective)

28. Focus on student strengths. (effective)

29. Appear to love teaching. (effective)

30. Act as though teaching is a chore. (ineffective)

31. Complain a lot. (ineffective)

32. Collaborate with co-workers in order to improve effectiveness. (effective)

33. Do whatever it takes to help a student succeed. (effective)

34. Believe that all students are capable and treat them accordingly. (effective)

35. Refuse to give up on any student. (effective)

Add as many of your own items to this test as you'd like. Because this is given as a "group test," all will do well. So now you can say, *Great job! You aced that test. I knew you would. But if we are brutally honest with ourselves, we can probably all find a few ways in which we are sometimes ineffective.*

IMPLEMENTATION

Give each teacher a copy (complete with answer key) of the test you just gave. Their assignment this week is to identify two or three areas of weakness in their own teaching and begin, this week, to improve in those areas. Ask them about their progress when you meet with them in the upcoming week. Make a special effort, of course, to speak with your least effective teachers, asking about the skills they're targeting and expressing your belief that their improvements will yield positive results. You might also make a special effort to speak with your best teachers and say, "I don't know how you found anything to work on, because you possess all of the effective teaching characteristics on that list. Don't think I don't recognize that!"

Notes

_____
_____
_____
_____
_____
_____
_____
_____
_____
_____
_____
_____
_____
_____
_____
_____
_____
_____
_____
_____
_____
_____
_____
_____
_____
_____
_____
_____
_____
_____
_____
_____
_____
_____
_____

Effective Teaching, Part 2

PURPOSE

In Inservice 9, "Effective Teaching, Part 1," you helped your teachers distinguish between effective and ineffective teaching. This week, you will help cement their understanding of the characteristics that separate effective from ineffective teachers. Is there a middle ground, a gray area between effective and ineffective teaching? Yes, there is. And it would represent great progress if you could get teachers whose teaching is ineffective to enter that gray area. The ultimate goal, of course, is to help all your teachers reach their true potential and become highly effective. But as we discussed in the introduction to this book, your primary goal should not be to make every teacher perfect but rather to help all of them become more effective than they already are. If you can succeed in doing that, you will see a dramatic improvement in student achievement.

It is an undeniable fact that teacher effectiveness is one of the most critical factors influencing student achievement. The better the teachers are, the more the students achieve—plainly, simply, unequivocally. Therefore, don't underestimate the power of these ten-minute inservices. If you're providing the training and following up on the assignments, teaching is going to improve in your school, ten minutes at a time. Now let's spend ten more minutes improving teaching, and therefore learning.

INSERVICE

Remind your teachers that in the previous inservice, they identified characteristics of both effective and ineffective teachers. They then identified a few of their own areas of weakness and began working on improving in those areas. Tell them that today you will allow them to work with partners to discuss how both effective and ineffective teachers might handle given situations in their classrooms.

Have each teacher choose a partner. If there is an uneven number, put three people together. Provide the following scenarios:

Effective Versus Ineffective Teaching Practices

- A student is constantly tattling on other students. The tattling is obsessive, and it needs to stop. Describe how an ineffective teacher might handle this. Describe how an effective teacher might handle this.

- A student is constantly making noises in class. The noises are aggravating everyone. Describe an ineffective teacher's response. Describe an effective teacher's response.

- A student is refusing to turn in any of her homework assignments. What might an ineffective teacher do? What might an effective teacher do?

- A student is chronically talking in class. She talks while the teacher is speaking, she talks during independent assignments, she talks when everyone is supposed to be quiet on the way to lunch, and so on. Describe how an ineffective teacher might handle this, and then how an effective teacher might handle it.

- The school is adopting a new program, and no one knows how effective it will be—or how ineffective. Its implementation will require training and hard work on the part of the teachers. Describe how the ineffective teacher and the effective teacher might each meet the challenges of this new program.

[Feel free to add your own scenarios to our list, perhaps addressing specific problems that your own teachers are facing.]

_____

_____

_____

_____

_____

_____

_____

_____

_____

_____

At this point, you might choose to leave the teachers to complete these assignments with their partners.

IMPLEMENTATION

Assign one or two teachers to collect the answers of all the pairs and then compile those answers into one document. Make sure each teacher receives a copy. Now each teacher has many new ideas and strategies for dealing with typical situations in more effective ways. And, just as important, many teachers might finally recognize that some of the ways they've been handling situations have been ineffective. Yet again, you've helped add substance to their ever-growing bags of tricks.

Notes

_____
_____
_____
_____
_____
_____
_____
_____
_____
_____
_____
_____
_____
_____
_____
_____
_____
_____
_____
_____
_____
_____
_____
_____
_____
_____
_____
_____
_____
_____

Inservice 11

Bell-to-Bell Teaching

PURPOSE

If you're going to walk into your most effective teacher's classroom one minute from now, you don't have to be psychic to predict that all students will be busily engaged in some type of learning activity. They won't necessarily all be engaged in the *same* activity, but they'll all be engaged. You can be certain, in advance, that no student will be sitting around with nothing to do.

Conversely, if you are going to walk into your least effective teacher's classroom one minute from now, you don't have to be psychic to predict that *not* all students will be engaged in some type of learning activity. You know, in advance, that some students will be sitting around with nothing to do. Those with nothing to do will either be sleeping or misbehaving. They certainly won't be sitting there, well behaved, patiently waiting until all the other students finish what they're doing or the teacher decides to move on to the next activity. Students are only human.

How is it possible to predict these scenarios before you even walk into the teachers' rooms? Because you know that only your best teachers are teaching and keeping students engaged from bell to bell. There's not a wasted moment. There is no time when a student finds herself with nothing to do. And this is one of the key reasons that these teachers rarely have discipline problems.

So how do effective teachers manage to keep students busy from bell to bell? They plan their lessons so that there's no wasted time. They plan activities that are engaging and as brief as possible (knowing that it is difficult to hold anyone's attention for a long period of time). They plan activities for early finishers. They plan remediation activities for students who may be struggling. Yes, teaching is a juggling act. There never has been and never will be a one-size-fits-all approach—at least not a successful one.

Less effective teachers give an assignment (which is usually not well thought out in regard to student interest and engagement) and assume it will take approximately twenty minutes for students to complete. Again, you don't have to be psychic to predict that some students will finish in five minutes, some will actually take five minutes to even get started, and some will never be able to finish in twenty minutes; and that throughout the allotted twenty minutes, there will be behavior problems. The teacher will be warning students to get busy. Several students will be saying they don't understand. Those who have finished will become bored and begin searching for distractions.

INSERVICE

Because this is only a ten-minute inservice, you'll want to identify just a few key strategies to help teachers engage their students from bell to bell. You will be speaking in future inservices about ways to engage students and ways to spice up lessons, but we want to keep this one short, informative, and doable. Its goal is twofold: (1) to help make teachers aware of what happens when students are allowed time with nothing to do, and (2) to suggest a few ways to plan for bell-to-bell teaching.

Begin by asking a series of questions:

- Have you ever given your students an assignment and had everyone finish at the same time?

- Have you ever noticed that the longer the assignment, the longer it takes some students to get started?

- Have you ever noticed that some students get started immediately and usually finish early?

- Have you ever noticed that some students don't seem to be able to finish the assignment in the allotted time?

- Have you ever noticed that as the assignment progresses, behavior problems seem to increase? For example, some students are asking what to do when they finish, some who should be working are misbehaving, and some are claiming they don't understand.

- Have you ever had a few minutes remaining before the bell rings and said something like, "If you can be quiet, I won't give you anything else to do"? What happened?

- Have you ever finished your lesson sooner than you had anticipated and then attempted to give your students some type of "busy work" to fill the time? How did your students respond?

Next, say the following:

We've all experienced some of what we've just discussed. And we all know that when students have time on their hands with nothing to do, they always find something to do. What they find to do, however, is almost never constructive.

One of the problems many teachers face with classroom management is the mismanagement of time. The best classroom managers share a secret—they make every effort to avoid any situation in which students are left with idle time. They teach and keep students engaged from bell to bell, from the moment the students enter the class until the moment they leave.

Give each teacher a copy of the following and read over all five suggestions with them:

Five Ways to Teach from Bell to Bell

1. Overplan. In other words, plan enough activities (meaningful ones, not time fillers) so that you will have more than you can teach in one lesson. Do this for every lesson you plan.

2. Start teaching and engaging students the moment they enter your class. Keep teaching and engaging them until they leave.

3. Plan for short, interesting activities. If you have to give an assignment, such as a writing assignment, that may take more than five or ten minutes for students to complete, break that assignment into parts and guide them through each part. At the very least, give them quick stretch breaks during the assignment. Remember, though, that short, quick activities hold students' interest better than those that are drawn out over longer periods of time.

4. When you give an assignment to students, have a plan for early finishers. Also, always be prepared to provide remediation for any student who might struggle with the activity.

5. Be prepared. Having your lesson well thought out and your materials organized and ready to go will allow you to move quickly and effectively from one activity to the next, without creating idle time.

IMPLEMENTATION

Now send your teachers off to implement those five ways to teach from bell to bell. This week and beyond, as you walk through classrooms, notice any improvement in your teachers' time management, and comment on it. If any teacher is still struggling, do what effective leaders do and provide immediate remediation.

Tell your teachers that you will be walking into classrooms looking specifically for the implementation of the five elements you have just shared. Your effective teachers will always be happy to have you visit their rooms and more than eager to receive suggestions for improvement. Your struggling teachers will now be more likely to be on their toes (as opposed to seated at their desks), working to improve their time management. And if they're not, it's time to remediate.

Notes

_____
_____
_____
_____
_____
_____
_____
_____
_____
_____
_____
_____
_____
_____
_____
_____
_____
_____
_____
_____
_____
_____
_____
_____
_____
_____
_____
_____
_____
_____
_____
_____

Teaching with Enthusiasm

PURPOSE

Walk up to any student on the campus and ask, "Does your teacher love teaching?" What will that student answer? We're going to boldly predict that you are thinking, "Well, it depends on who his teacher is!" Are there some teachers on the faculty who always seem to love what they do? Are there those who only occasionally appear to like what they do? And are there those who act as though what they do is a daily chore?

The bottom line is that teachers are actors. *All* true professionals have to be actors, because no one always feels professional or enthusiastic. It should never be an option for any teacher to appear anything less than enthusiastic about teaching. The key word here is "appear." None of us always feels enthusiastic, but we all have to appear that way. Fake it if you have to. (And yes, you do often have to!)

Today you'll be auditioning your teachers. How much enthusiasm can they sustain?

INSERVICE

Begin by discussing how teaching involves performing and how teachers in many ways have to be actors. Then say, *Imagine that you are an actor in a Broadway play, performing every evening. Should your performances become weaker and less enthusiastic as Friday approaches? Of course not, because each performance is as important as the last or the next. How can you justify giving your Tuesday night audience a bad performance, just because you had a bad day on Tuesday? They want you to* act.

Continue discussing the fact that as teachers, we too are actors. And we have to be exceptionally good actors if we want to reach and teach our students. It's all too easy to forget this and become a little (or a lot) too human with our students.

It's not that we, as educators, should pretend to be superhuman. But we should never appear human in a way that is anything short of caring, compassionate, enthusiastic, committed, and professional.

If anyone were to ask your students if you love teaching and enjoy your time with them each day, what would they answer? If you're thinking that some of them might not answer with an enthusiastic "Yes!" then it's time to polish your acting skills.

Offer your teachers the following ideas (and ask them to add a few of their own) for teaching with enthusiasm:

- Start each lesson telling students how excited you are about what they will be learning today.

- Express your love of teaching to your students often.

- Act as though everything you teach is the most exciting thing you have ever taught.

- Celebrate the successes of your students as they learn new skills or accomplish tasks.

- When you are not feeling enthusiastic, fake it.

- Use such key phrases as "Wait until you see what we'll be doing today," "I can hardly wait to get started on today's lesson," "This activity is going to be so interesting and fun," or "Isn't this amazing?"

Say to your teachers, *When you're teaching students, your enthusiasm becomes their enthusiasm, and your lack of it becomes their lack of it. That's why we all need to work at being as enthusiastic as possible in our classrooms (and on the campus) every day. I'm working at being more enthusiastic, too.*

IMPLEMENTATION

The assignment for your teachers is to go back to their classrooms and practice their acting skills. Tell them that although you know and respect the fact that they all have their own personality and teaching style, you want to see a few commonalities in their teaching. You want them all to appear to love everything they are teaching. You want them all to think of themselves as actors on a stage, giving their best performance every day. You want them to appear enthusiastic in the classroom, even if they are having a bad day.

Notes

_____
_____
_____
_____
_____
_____
_____
_____
_____
_____
_____
_____
_____
_____
_____
_____
_____
_____

Teaching Like a Great Coach

PURPOSE

Have you ever watched a great coach in action? It's poetry in motion. Great coaches are great teachers. Their lesson plans (game plans) are always evolving; they'd never dream of using the same game plan over and over, because they know that what works with this year's team may not work with next year's team. Great coaches make each player aware of his strengths and his weaknesses. But they don't focus on the weaknesses; instead, they develop plans to help each player overcome them. The coaches' main focus, though, remains on the players' strengths. Great coaches work tirelessly, far beyond the normal working hours, to make the most of each player's strengths. They know the value of procedures and practice them over and over with their players. Great coaches are always writing and delivering motivational speeches, because they know that players need daily doses of inspiration. They teach players of all ability levels, so there's no such thing as one-size-fits-all coaching. They never sit still: when they are in the presence of their players, they are walking around constantly, monitoring, encouraging, coaching, teaching, and remediating. A great coach will never be found sitting at his desk on the sideline. He has a desk in his office, but he uses it only when the players are not around. On game day, he's pacing back and forth, watching every move his players make. No, he can't go onto the field and play the game for them. He has prepared them and must now let them play. But he's watching constantly, offering encouragement and guidance. When something stops working, a great coach calls a time-out and reteaches or redirects.

Do you see where we're going with this? Great coaches are great teachers, and great teachers are great coaches. Their content and their arenas may differ, but the coaching and teaching processes are remarkably similar. Are your teachers great coaches?

INSERVICE

Begin this inservice by asking, *How many of you have ever watched a football game?* (We always use the example of football, because it's a prevalent sport. Even people who are not sports fans have seen a game of football being played, so everyone will be able to relate.)

Next, ask the following questions, leading your teachers to draw parallels between great teaching and great coaching:

- Do great coaches have lesson plans? (Yes.) What do they call their lesson plans? (Game plans.)

- Are the same game plans used over and over every year? (No. The same game plans may not work well with next year's team. Coaches do keep some of what works for future game plans, however.)

- Do great coaches practice procedures with their players? (Yes. They practice procedures every day of the entire season, over and over and over.)

- During practice, what are great coaches doing? (Teaching, walking around, working with groups, working with individual players, guiding, remediating, reteaching, encouraging, and so on.)

- Do great coaches work with players who all have equal athletic and intellectual abilities? (No.)

- If a great coach has a player who is struggling with one particular skill, what does the coach do? (He spends time helping that player improve.)

- Are the players made aware of their strengths and weaknesses by the great coach? (Yes.)

- Does the great coach ever sit at his desk on the sidelines during practice or during a game? (No.)

- Where is the coach's desk, and when does he use it? (It's in his office, and he uses it to write his plans and complete paperwork when the players are not around.)

- Do great coaches serve as motivators? (Yes.)

- Do great coaches write motivational speeches to deliver to players? (Yes.) What's the purpose of these speeches, and when are they typically delivered? (The purpose is to get the players excited about the game or the next play and to motivate them to do their best. The speeches typically occur right before practice begins, during practice, right before a game, and during a game. They also occur after practice and after games.)

- Do great coaches focus more on player strengths or player weaknesses? (Strengths.)

- During a game, does everything always go as the great coach has planned? (No.)

- When something stops working during the game, what does a great coach do? (He calls a time-out and reteaches or changes his strategy or gives a little pep talk.)

- Do great coaches often express how much they believe in their players? (Yes.)

Now ask the following:

- Do great teachers have game plans? (Yes.) What do they call their game plans? (Lesson plans.)

- Are the same lesson plans used over and over every year? (No. The same lesson plan may not work well with next year's students. Teachers do keep some of what works for future lesson plans, however.)

- Do great teachers practice procedures with their students? (Yes. They practice procedures every day of the entire school year, over and over and over.)

- During class time, what are great teachers doing? (Teaching, walking around, working with groups, working with individual students, guiding, remediating, reteaching, encouraging, and so on.)

- Do great teachers teach students who all have equal abilities? (No.)

- If a great teacher has one student who is struggling with one skill, what does the teacher do? (He spends time helping that student improve.)

- Are the students made aware of their strengths and weaknesses by the great teacher? (Yes.)

- Does the great teacher ever sit at his desk during class time? (This one may lead to interesting discussion. Here is your opportunity to explain that teachers, unlike coaches, do not have separate offices. Their classrooms double as their offices when the students are not there. It is a rare occurrence to see a great teacher seated at her desk during class time. Even during tests, great teachers are constantly walking around and monitoring students.)

- Do great teachers serve as motivators? (Yes.)

- Do great teachers write motivational speeches to deliver to their students? (Yes.) What's the purpose of these speeches, and when are they typically delivered? (The purpose is to get the students excited about the lesson or skill and to motivate them to do their best. The speeches typically occur right before class begins, during class, right before a new activity, and during activities. They also occur at the end of class.)

- Do great teachers focus more on student strengths or student weaknesses? (Strengths.)

- During a lesson, does everything always go as the great teacher has planned? (No.)

- When something stops working during a lesson or activity, what does a great teacher do? (He takes a time-out and reteaches or changes his strategy or gives a little pep talk.)

- Do great teachers often express how much they believe in their students? (Yes.)

IMPLEMENTATION

Ask your teachers, *So what's the difference between great coaches and great teachers, aside from the fact that their content is different and their arenas are different?* Spend a few minutes allowing them to discuss the question and determine that there is very little difference. Great coaching is great teaching, and vice versa.

Send your teachers back to their classrooms with the task of teaching more like great coaches. Tell them you'll be listening for their pep talks, and you'll be watching for active "coaching" in their classrooms. Ask each of them to be prepared to tell you, during your observations or your upcoming discussions with them, how they are working on improving their coaching skills in the classroom.

Notes

_____
_____
_____
_____
_____
_____
_____
_____
_____
_____
_____
_____
_____
_____
_____
_____
_____
_____
_____

Inservice 14

Be Here, There, and Everywhere

PURPOSE

If you were to go into a classroom and ask the students, "Where does your teacher usually stand?" could they tell you? In some classrooms, might the students be able to identify the exact spot where their teacher can almost always be found? Think about it. When you go to a meeting, do you usually sit in a particular place in the room? Maybe you sit in the back row on the aisle. Maybe you sit about halfway to the front, to the left of the center aisle. Are you a front-row person? Most people gravitate toward particular areas in a room. Notice at your faculty meetings that most teachers have claimed their territory! They always sit in the same place, and everyone knows not to sit in that place because it belongs to So-and-So. Correct?

People tend to establish their own comfort zones. They become creatures of habit because they are comfortable with their habits. This is fine if someone is going to a meeting and simply feels more comfortable sitting in a certain area of the room. It becomes a problem, however, when a teacher tends to stay in one spot or in one particular area in a classroom. In these cases, behavior problems almost always occur farthest away from the teacher. Many teachers tend to spend most of their time in the front of the classroom. Why do you think so many students scurry to claim the back-row seats? They know that the farther they are from the teacher, the more they can misbehave.

The fact is that if you ask a student where her teacher usually stands, she should not be able to answer that question. We often hear teachers say, "My students get nervous if I walk around. They don't like it when I hover over them too much." That statement tells you that you are dealing with a teacher who rarely leaves his designated area. So when he does leave and decides to walk around, the students find it odd, and they react accordingly.

INSERVICE

Begin the inservice by saying, *I'd like to share an observation. I've noticed that* _____ *sits in that same chair for every faculty meeting. I've noticed that* _____ *sits in his same chair also.* Point out as many as you can, taking care to do this tactfully and somewhat tongue in cheek. Your teachers will get a laugh out of this. Next ask, *Why do so many of you sit in the same place every time?* After a brief discussion, ask, *If someone were to walk into your classroom and ask your students where you typically stand, could the students point to a general area of the room?* Make it clear that you don't want them to answer this aloud, as it is definitely not your intention to embarrass anyone. You simply want them to think about the question you have just asked. Discuss the importance of movement around the room. (As the leader of this activity, you should also model the same expected behavior, moving around the room as you deliver the inservice.)

Next, share the following:

In the classrooms of effective teachers, you simply cannot guess where the teacher will be next. Students are comfortable with the fact that the teacher walks around the room, because they are accustomed to it. These teachers, by the way, are not just walking around randomly. There's always a method to their madness. However, they move around so much and their actions are so subtle that the students never figure out the reason for the teacher's being in a particular place at a particular time. For instance, let's say that during a class discussion, the teacher notices that Andrew is off task. She doesn't stare at him, she doesn't warn him, and she doesn't make any attempt to embarrass him. She just happens to end up right next to him. Ninety-nine times out of a hundred, Andrew starts paying attention. He doesn't know whether his teacher noticed that he was off task or not, because it's not strange for her to be standing next to him. Maybe she saw him, maybe she didn't, but the result is that he gets back on task.

Let's contrast that with a less effective teacher. Given the same scenario, a less effective teacher, upon noticing that Andrew is off task, might first warn him to get back on task. If he doesn't comply, she might head over to his desk. This is almost always done in a threatening way. So of course he is uncomfortable with his teacher hovering over him and staring at him. And he's uncomfortable with the fact that everyone knows what the teacher is doing. Game on! Ninety-nine times out of a hundred, Andrew engages in some sort of power struggle with the teacher.

IMPLEMENTATION

You are now asking your teachers to step out of their comfort zones and become more aware of, and more skilled at, engaging in purposeful movement around the room. Tell them that for the next several days, you'll be observing for increased (and purposeful) teacher movement around the room. You may choose to leave them with the following poem:

Our Teacher Is Always Everywhere

Our teacher moves around the room; all over the place she goes
Where will she be headed next? No one really knows
She's here, she's there, she's everywhere, she's constantly walking around
If you close your eyes, you cannot guess where next she will be found
She's helping me, she's helping you, she's monitoring everything we do
She's over here, she's over there. Our teacher is always everywhere!

Notes

_____
_____
_____
_____
_____
_____
_____
_____
_____
_____
_____
_____
_____
_____
_____
_____
_____
_____
_____
_____
_____
_____
_____
_____
_____
_____
_____
_____
_____
_____
_____

Making Lessons Meaningful

PURPOSE

We all hear it over and over . . . if lessons are meaningful to students, they will want to participate and will be more likely to connect with the material or skills. This improves their chances of learning and succeeding. There's no controversy in education regarding the importance of teaching in a way that facilitates a connection between the subject matter and the life experiences of students. We all know that this is important. We all know that it works. So why aren't we all doing it?

Remember that many teachers teach the way they were taught. That can be good or bad, depending on how they were taught. But many, many teachers continue to teach in ways that are not effective in today's world. For some, it's all they know. Others are aware that there's a more effective way, yet it's difficult for them to leave their comfort zones. Today you'll be helping all your teachers take some new risks, rethink what meaningful learning entails, and make their lessons even better than they currently are.

INSERVICE

Begin by leading a brief discussion based on the following questions and ideas:

- Is it important that the lessons you teach hold meaning for your students?
- Are you interested in learning about things that hold no meaning for you? For instance, if you are a first-year teacher and you learn that there is a meeting after school today regarding teachers' retirement, will you be motivated to attend? No? But what if the speaker at the meeting is excellent? Still not interested? Technically, this could affect you thirty years down the road. But isn't it true that you can't even concern yourself with things a year ahead right now? Chances are good that you won't be attending this meeting.
- Would you agree that any one of us is more likely to pay attention and give our best efforts to a task that holds personal meaning or value?
- What are some approaches you take in your own teaching to ensure that learning is meaningful to your students? (Let them share a few ideas.)

Next, have your teachers decide which of these lessons or activities would likely hold more meaning for their students:

1. An activity that asks students to underline the nouns in given sentences
   or
   An activity that asks students to attempt to speak without using any nouns

2. A lesson in which the teacher has students study the definitions of Newton's laws of motion
   or
   A lesson in which the teacher and students study and discuss how the laws of motion apply to football or to playing video games

3. Listening to a lecture about a historical figure, taking notes, and then being tested on facts about that person
   or

Conducting research to compare the historical figure to themselves, predicting how that person would act if he lived in our world today or determining how that figure actually did impact life as students know it today

4. An activity in which students study probability by rolling a given set of dice
or
An activity in which students use probability (as it relates to meteorology) to determine which month or week would be best to have an outdoor class party

Now have teachers share four or five meaningful learning activities they are currently incorporating in their lessons.

1. _____
_____
_____

2. _____
_____
_____

3. _____
_____
_____

4. _____
_____
_____

5. _____
_____
_____

Thank them for sharing. Be sure to express enthusiasm for their creative ideas. By doing this, you are validating those who are willing to contribute and share their ideas, and you are helping make less effective teachers aware that what they are doing might not be effective.

IMPLEMENTATION

Pair teachers of like subject areas and give them the following assignment:

Discuss, with your partner, ideas for five new ways of taking lessons that you already teach and making them more meaningful to the lives of your students. When you have come up with five, add them to the master document that will be posted online. Be sure to post your ideas by [date].

Note: If you don't want to post the document online, then simply tell the teachers where the master copy will be located so that they can add their ideas by the deadline.

If you think their bags of tricks are getting bulky, we can hardly wait for you to conduct Inservice 16, "Fifty Ways to Make Learning Fun."

Notes

_____

_____

_____

_____

_____

_____

_____

_____

_____

_____

_____

_____

_____

_____

_____

_____

_____

_____

Inservice 16

Fifty Ways to Make Learning Fun

PURPOSE

In the previous inservice, we discussed the importance of making learning meaningful. Today we're going to focus on taking meaningful learning and making it fun! People of all ages learn best when they are in a positive emotional state, when they see a task as meaningful, and when learning something new is actually fun. It stands to reason that if you enjoy something, you're going to want to engage in doing it. If you don't enjoy it, you'll avoid it.

You can take almost any concept and teach it in a way that is boring. You can take almost any concept and teach it in a way that is fun. Which would you choose as a learner—the boring way or the fun way? We continue to learn that many teachers would like to liven up their teaching, but simply don't know how. They realize that the old "lecture–read the chapter–answer the questions at the end of the chapter–copy notes–memorize notes" technique is not fun for anyone.

It's also not effective. But many of them don't know what else to do. Again, it is true that many teachers simply teach the way they were taught.

Do you have a few teachers who may be in a rut, lacking in creative ideas for making learning more fun for their students (and making teaching more fun for themselves)? Rest assured that today's inservice will spark new life in *all* your teachers. No longer will they lack ideas for ways to make learning more enjoyable.

INSERVICE

Begin the inservice with a brief discussion of the importance of making learning fun for students. Then tell your teachers that today they will be creating a list of fifty ways to make learning fun for students. To spark their creativity, provide them with a few examples of ways to make learning more fun:

Making Learning Fun—Examples

- Compare story characters or historical figures to people students know.
- Incorporate short video clips into lessons.
- Involve students in role-play activities.
- Turn content into songs or allow students to create their own songs related to the content.
- Create stories or plays.
- Read to your students.
- Take online field trips.
- Let them go on virtual vacations and then report to the class about them.
- Take field trips on your own campus.
- Send students on treasure hunts in the classroom and have them search for clues to solve problems.
- Play learning games based on game shows.
- Allow students to teach one another.
- Have friendly competition in which teams of students race to solve problems or find answers.
- Let them make their own videos.

- Perform experiments.
- Have them interview community members and share those interviews with the class.
- Invite community members into the classroom as guest speakers.
- Have contests in which students create their own learning games.
- Incorporate technology into practically anything.
- Communicate online with students in other states or countries.

We've shared a few broad suggestions, but you will want your teachers to be more specific in their descriptions of ideas. For example, a teacher might share that when she is teaching grammar, she has students close their eyes, and she begins speaking. Every time she makes a grammatical error (which she does intentionally), the students are to raise their hands.

Because this inservice is only ten minutes, you might choose to do the following:

- Get them started compiling the list and then leave them on their own to finish

  or

- Send all of them off with the task of emailing a designated teacher with two ideas for the list. We recommend having each teacher provide two ideas in case some offer the same idea. The designated teacher will compile a list of fifty and send it to you. You can then ensure that all teachers receive a copy.

Share this inservice idea with a principal or staff developer in a neighboring school. After his or her teachers come up with a list of fifty, exchange lists. Your teachers will now have a list of one hundred ways to make learning fun.

IMPLEMENTATION

Have every teacher send you an email telling you about one new strategy (gained from this inservice) that she will be incorporating into her teaching this week. Tell them all to include the day and time they will be using it. Let them know that you will be stopping by some of their classrooms to enjoy watching the students participate in this new activity. No, you can't make it to every teacher's class-room. You don't have to. **You know where you need to be**. At the end of the week, have every teacher send you an email telling you how the new activity went. One short paragraph is plenty. You don't have to read every email. **You know which ones you need to read**.

By doing this, you have guaranteed that every one of your teachers has at least attempted to make learning more fun for students this week. In future obser-vations, when you encounter a teacher whose lesson is lacking in fun, refer to the list and suggest one or more of the activities.

Once again, one ten-minute inservice has led to better teaching and improved student learning in every classroom. Some of your teachers, of course, will take that list of fifty ways to make learning fun and try every single one. But at the very least, if everyone tries at least one, you've made a difference.

Notes

_____

_____

_____

_____

_____

_____

_____

_____

_____

_____

_____

_____

_____

_____

_____

_____

_____

PART 3

Improving
School Climate

Getting Parents Involved

PURPOSE

We hear the same remarks over and over: "The parents just won't get involved. And the older the students get, the less the parents participate." There is, in fact, some truth to this—unless, of course, you go to a sporting event. Many parents come out to watch their children participate in the big game, don't they? They bring the grandparents, the little brothers and sisters, sometimes even the neighbors. So let's capitalize on that. Let's work at getting parents as excited to come to Back to School Night as they are to attend sporting events.

Today's inservice is an opportunity to change the way your teachers invite parents to Back to School Night. We've seen this technique work in many, many schools—usually to the amazement of the teachers. Remember, even if you get only a handful of parents who don't typically attend these events to show up this year, it's more than worth the effort.

INSERVICE

Begin by sharing the following true story:

> *A high school was preparing for its annual Back to School Night. During the faculty meeting, the teachers were complaining, saying that it was a waste of time to even host such an event because so few parents ever attended. And, they claimed, the parents who did attend were not the parents who needed to attend.*
>
> *The principal suggested that they approach this year's invitations differently. Typically, a letter of invitation went out to all parents. Typically, the turnout was dismal. "This year," the principal said, "every homeroom teacher will make a simple phone call to each student's parents, personally inviting them to our event." The teachers were skeptical but willing. The principal gave them a script, telling them exactly what to say to the parents. If no one answered, the teacher was not expected to continue trying to reach the parent. Instead, the teacher was simply to leave a message, enthusiastically inviting the parents to Back to School Night. And oh yes, there was mention of door prizes and good food.*
>
> *The end result? So many parents attended the high school's Back to School Night that the staff had to scramble to find enough chairs to accommodate them. The event was treated like a pep rally, with the teachers letting parents know how excited they were to be teaching this year's students. Positive aspects of the school were featured. Parents were treated like guests at a party. They left the event feeling good and proud and welcomed by the teachers and administrators. Many left with prizes, and all left with full stomachs. Those who did not attend soon heard about what they had missed from the parents who did attend. Back to School Night was the talk of the town!*

After sharing this story, discuss the real goals of Back to School Night: getting parents excited about the school and the upcoming school year, and making sure they feel welcome at the school. This event is basically your chance to make a great first impression. And when parents have a positive impression of the school, they are more likely to participate in their children's education—which makes your job much, much easier.

Why *don't* more parents attend Back to School Nights? For one or more of the following reasons:

- The event lasts too long.
- The parents feel intimidated by some of the faculty and staff.
- Teachers are talking about content that many of the parents don't understand.
- There are no refreshments or door prizes that could entice people to attend. (Yes, even adults like good food and cool prizes!)
- The event is just not fun.

Tell your teachers that this year, you'll be approaching Back to School Night differently. The event will look like the one you just described in your story. Teachers will be asked to call the parents of each student in their homeroom. Read a suggested script (and make sure teachers leave with a copy, in case they want to use it).

Back to School Night Invitation

Hi. This is [name of teacher], your [son's/daughter's] homeroom [or grade-level] teacher. I'm so happy to be teaching [name of student] this year, and I'm excited to invite you to our Back to School Night next [day] at [time]. It will be a short and fun event, and we'll be serving wonderful refreshments. We'll also be giving out some great door prizes. I just wanted to personally invite you. I hope to meet you in person next [day]!

Tell teachers that if no one answers, they may feel free to leave a message including all these details and extending a warm invitation.

IMPLEMENTATION

Now for the planning of your new and improved Back to School Night. First, delegate. Have a few of your best teachers help plan the event. Your best teachers are, by definition, wonderful planners; take advantage of those skills.

Tailor the event to your own school and community, of course. Just make sure that there are refreshments and door prizes and that the event showcases your school and makes the parents feel welcome. Have someone greeting parents as they enter the school. And keep the event short and simple! All parents should leave excited about the upcoming year and confident that their precious children are in the capable hands of excellent, caring, dedicated professionals.

There is no downside to giving this a try. You have nothing to lose and only parental support to gain. As we noted earlier, if even a few more parents attend, your efforts have paid off. And those who don't attend will soon hear of the event and its success, so they too will have a good first impression of the school and the upcoming school year.

On a final note, encourage your teachers to talk up the event in their classrooms, making sure that students are getting the message (and, you hope, delivering it to their parents) that Back to School Night is the place to be!

Notes

_____
_____
_____
_____
_____
_____
_____
_____
_____
_____

Greeting Students Daily

PURPOSE

Why is it that when you step onto an airplane, enter a restaurant, or walk into Walmart, you are greeted by someone who seems delighted that you've arrived? It's because happy customers who feel valued are more likely to buy what is being sold—and to want to come back.

It is vital that students believe that their teachers are happy to see them every day, and today's inservice will help cement that point. When you have all the adults in a school convincing all the students that they are welcome and wanted, behavior improves instantly and dramatically. When behavior improves, so does achievement. It truly is that simple. But we have yet to find even one school where all the teachers greet all their students every day.

Make your school the first.

INSERVICE

As your teachers arrive for today's faculty meeting, be standing at the door with a giant smile on your face. Greet them all individually, making it clear that you are elated to see them. As they enter, thank them for coming to the meeting. And if this is not something you typically do, be prepared to see shock on their faces.

You're about to use that shock, and their other reactions, to make your inservice more effective.

Begin by discussing what a difference a smile can make. Smiling lets your students know that you're happy to have them in your classroom; it makes them feel special and wanted. A teacher's smile can be contagious for even the most disaffected student. A teacher who smiles at every student every day is saying, "I'm happy you're here, I'm happy to be teaching you, and this is a safe, pleasant environment." These kinds of environments promote optimal learning and improved behavior.

After you've discussed the power of a smile, discuss with your teachers why Walmart hires a professional greeter to welcome each customer and why the best hosts make every guest feel special. It's because people who feel that you are happy to see them and want them in your establishment are much more likely to buy what you are selling.

Tell the teachers that it is no different with students. Students are our customers. We are "selling" them the specific content of the curriculum, and we're also "selling" them a thirst for learning. Students who believe that we are genuinely happy to see them each day are much more likely to "buy" what we're selling. And, sadly, for some students, school is the only place where adults are happy to see them.

Establish the very important fact that standing at your door each day when the students arrive does not necessarily constitute "greeting." A teacher standing at her door saying, "Come on in. Hurry and get busy. Your work is on the board. Let's go. The bell is about to ring . . . " is not greeting students. It sounds more like "Welcome to my torture chamber!"

Demonstrate what an effective greeting looks like. Show the teachers how to stand at the door with a huge smile on their faces (as you did today when they entered the meeting). Suggest remarks they might make:

- Hi, how are you?

- I'm happy to see you!

- Thanks for coming to class.
- I can't wait to show you what we're going to be doing in class today!
- Tim, I'm so glad you're back. I missed you yesterday.
- I *love* your new haircut.

Tell teachers: *The key to successful greeting is to show your students that you're elated to see them every day and that you miss them when they leave you. If you can convince students that you feel this way about them, you will see their behavior improve immediately. You will also notice that they're much more willing to participate in class. The happier you appear—even if you're exhausted or feeling cranky—the happier your students will be!*

IMPLEMENTATION

You've greeted your teachers, you've established the importance of greeting students, and you've shown them what an effective greeting is—and what it's not. Now make the change happen. Tell teachers that they will notice your making an extra effort to greet students on the school grounds every day for the next week. Tell them that you want them to make that same sort of effort at the beginning and end of every class period for the next week. Say you'll be walking the halls, enjoying the sight of them greeting their students with newfound enthusiasm. Then tell them you will bring them all back together in a week so that you can all share your greeting experiences.

When you do bring them back together, spend a few minutes sharing what reactions you noticed as you greeted the students all week. Then allow teachers to share what they noticed. Tell them you want this practice to continue for the rest of the year. Greeting students enthusiastically every day is a simple way to say you care, you're happy to see them, you love teaching them, and you want them to return. It's also a quick, easy, free way to improve student behavior!

It is now your job, of course, to continue to promote the greeting of students every day for the rest of the year. Continue to model the behavior, to notice it in others, and to praise teachers for greeting their students warmly. Make sure that your teachers feel that you're happy to see *them* every day, too!

If students arrive and leave on a happy note,
  better behavior and learning you're sure to promote!

Notes

A Kind Reminder

PURPOSE

It's all too common: teachers return from staff development workshops excited to try the new ideas and instructional strategies they learned, but their day-to-day work in the classroom is so busy and unrelenting that they don't find the time to try anything new. As the days wear on after the inservice, the details of those exciting new strategies become fuzzier and fuzzier in their memories. As educators, we have good intentions, but our follow-through is sometimes weak. The best inservice in the world is pointless if the new knowledge and skills are not put to use in the classroom.

As administrators and staff developers, you know it's not good enough to provide your teachers with great inservices. There has to be follow-through. But that follow-through doesn't have to be time-consuming. You're already observing teachers; so, as you do, be sure to look for signs that they're implementing the new skills they're learning, and comment on those accomplishments when you confer. When you meet a teacher in the hallway, ask how a particular new strategy is or is not working in the classroom. When you do your walk-throughs, remind teachers that you're looking for evidence of what they learned in the latest inservice. Encourage them to talk to each other about how the new strategies are working for them. And constantly remind them of all they have been learning!

The purpose of today's inservice is to do exactly that kind of review—to remind your teachers of all they have been learning and allow them to share their successes (and failures) with one another. For those teachers who haven't exactly been setting the world on fire with their efforts, this inservice will serve as a reminder of what they need to be doing. For those who actually *have* been setting the world on fire, this inservice will be a great way to pat them on the back and remind them of all their accomplishments.

INSERVICE

Begin the inservice by saying, *I'd like to give you a much-deserved pat on the back. Over the last few weeks, we've learned a lot together.* Tell the teachers how happy you are to see so many of them

- Greeting their students as they enter their classrooms every day
- Establishing a consistent way of securing students' attention
- Setting clear rules and procedures
- Being more consistent with their rules and procedures
- Using private practice sessions with certain students
- Engaging students from bell to bell

Add anything else you have observed:

- _____
- _____
- _____
- _____

Next, provide a few minutes for teachers to share any positive results they have enjoyed after using these strategies. If you have already noticed a drop in discipline referrals, even if it is from only a few teachers, share that happy news.

If some of your teachers still have not completely embraced the strategies you have been teaching through your inservices, take a few minutes to remind them of what you expect to see as you walk through the school and observe in classrooms.

What's most important, however, is to acknowledge the great progress many of your teachers are making and to thank them for their efforts. Anyone making *any* extra effort deserves to feel validated and appreciated. Those who have not put forth any effort will be feeling quite uncomfortable right about now—and that's exactly how you want them to feel!

IMPLEMENTATION

For the implementation phase of this inservice, assign each teacher to a partner teacher. Their assignment this week is to share with each other three things they have learned from the previous inservices and how they have implemented those insights in their classrooms. Be sure to pair effective teachers with less effective teachers.

We suggest that you have this type of reminder inservice every few weeks or as the need arises. Include any previous inservice topics about which you feel they need to be reminded.

Notes

_____

Inservice 20

Twenty-Five Reasons to Be Proud of Our School

PURPOSE

Isn't it easy to get bogged down with all that is negative? We've been trained to identify problems, and that skill can be a valuable asset. For instance, as educators, we are trained to recognize what is broken and create solutions to fix it. But all is not broken! Sometimes we get so involved in "fixing" that we forget to revel in what is working. This is an easy, and sometimes alluring, trap. Don't fall! And don't let your teachers fall, either. It is most definitely your job as a leader to fix problems. But it is also your job, and a most important one, to recognize what is working well for some and to use that knowledge to benefit others, mainly students and teachers.

Believe it or not, it is typically far easier for a teacher to list a student's weaknesses than it is to list his strengths. And sometimes it is easier for an administrator to list all that is wrong with the school than it is to list all that is right. Today we will help you and your teachers turn those tables.

On the following lines, list ten reasons to be proud of your school—including actions of teachers, actions of students, successful programs, successful strategies, recognition the school has received, activities in which the school is involved, and anything else you can think of.

1. _____
2. _____
3. _____
4. _____
5. _____
6. _____
7. _____
8. _____
9. _____
10. _____

Wouldn't you agree that the items you've listed are true and valid reasons to be proud? Feel free to list more, but we just wanted to make a point. We wanted to get you thinking about all that is good and right with your school.

We continue to notice that very few schools display a list of reasons to be proud of the school. Imagine walking into a school and being greeted by a list of some of the reasons the teachers and administrators are proud of the school. It is important for anyone who enters your school to immediately feel that yours is a positive environment, an environment where the adults in charge of the students take pride in what they do. Positive school environments are conducive to promoting better student achievement and behavior. Positive school environments are conducive to promoting better teaching and better teacher behavior. So let's get busy becoming more positive and displaying our pride in all the good that we do on a daily basis.

INSERVICE

Begin the inservice by discussing the following points:

- Teachers are trained to identify problems—problems with student behavior, with student achievement, with student abilities, and so on.

- Being able to identify problems is a skill worth possessing, as it is the first step in solving any problem.

- Because we are all human, it is sometimes easy to focus too heavily on what is wrong in our environments and ignore all that is right.

- The more you focus on what's good, the more good you will see.

Following this discussion, say to your teachers, *Today we are going to focus on all that is good and right with our school. Like you, I'm proud to be affiliated with this school, and I'm proud to know I'm making a difference in the lives of students. I've taken the time to list a few things I'm proud of regarding our school.* At this time, share the list you made in preparation for the inservice.

Next, have your teachers come up with twenty-five reasons they are proud of this school. Items might include the following:

- We treat every student with respect and dignity.

- We work hard to accommodate and celebrate the diverse needs of our students.

- We have an award-winning debate team.

- We have been recognized as _____

- Our teachers work tirelessly to ensure the success of every student.

- We're proud of _____, who is our Teacher of the Year.

- We're proud to have the privilege of teaching the best students anywhere!

- We're proud that our band has won the _____ Award.

- We're proud that our football team accomplished _____.

- We're proud that our _____ club received the _____ Award.

After allowing the teachers to brainstorm ideas, designate one person to condense those ideas into the following document.

DOWNLOAD

Twenty-Five Reasons We Are Proud of Our School

1. _____
2. _____
3. _____
4. _____
5. _____
6. _____
7. _____
8. _____
9. _____
10. _____
11. _____
12. _____
13. _____
14. _____
15. _____
16. _____
17. _____
18. _____
19. _____
20. _____
21. _____
22. _____
23. _____
24. _____
25. _____

With this one simple activity, you have helped remind teachers that what they do matters; you have encouraged them to consider all that is positive about the school; you have helped make your environment even more positive; you have created a simple way for everyone who enters the school to know what is good and right with the school; and you have created a daily reminder for students and teachers to continue to take pride in their school and in themselves. That's ten minutes well spent.

IMPLEMENTATION

Post this document prominently in the school, in every hallway and in every teacher's classroom if possible. Make sure that it is visible to visitors as they enter the school. If you'd like, have every teacher sign it at the bottom.

Notes

_____
_____
_____
_____
_____
_____
_____
_____
_____
_____
_____
_____
_____
_____
_____
_____
_____
_____

21

Student Appreciation Week

PURPOSE

In education, we dedicate days and even weeks to celebrating and appreciating people who make significant contributions to educating students. There's a Boss's Day and a Teacher Appreciation Week and lots of other days and weeks to celebrate people who work with students. But how many schools or school districts do you know of that take time to celebrate the one group that provides all of us with jobs? What about a Student Appreciation Week? A little appreciation goes a long way. If you don't believe that, try removing Teacher Appreciation Week from the calendar. (Don't worry; we're not suggesting that you do that. We're only asking you to imagine the ramifications.)

People have a basic need to feel appreciated. When they feel appreciated, they work harder, behave better, and bend over backwards to do their best. Wouldn't it be wonderful if there were a simple way to encourage students to work harder, behave better, and give their best? There is: appreciate them. Right about now, you may be thinking, "We do all kinds of things to show our appreciation to our students." Good. Keep doing those things. But along with whatever you're currently doing, consider declaring one week of the school year Student Appreciation Week.

INSERVICE

Tell your teachers that you will be designating one week as Student Appreciation Week. During this particular week, there will be a variety of activities to show appreciation to the students. The following are just a few ideas you may want to consider:

- Hold a special assembly where the teachers provide entertainment for the students.

- In the classroom, a different student every day gets to sit in the teacher's chair.

- One day, serve ice cream in the cafeteria.

- Have a dress-up day when students are allowed to dress like their teachers.

- Offer free admission to students for a sporting event.

- Have local businesses donate prizes for drawings.

- Have no homework all week.

- Add five minutes to recess or to a break in class.

- Post signs of appreciation around the school.

- Each day, feature one teacher during announcements who states reasons why he or she is grateful for students.

- Send a letter to all parents telling them how much you appreciate their children.

- Encourage teachers to have drawings for prizes each day in their classrooms.

- Encourage teachers to write thank-you notes to students.

- Each day of the week, have your teachers begin class by telling the students one or two things they appreciate about them.

- Host a student forum, allowing students to make suggestions on how to improve the school.

- Make badges for all teachers to wear all week that say, "I Appreciate My Students."

- As administrators, visit classrooms during the week just to tell the students they are appreciated.

Add your own and your teachers' ideas here:

_____

_____

_____

_____

_____

_____

_____

_____

_____

_____

_____

IMPLEMENTATION

Let the teachers run the show on this one. Designate a committee to be in charge of Student Appreciation Week. There are teachers on every faculty who love to orchestrate parties and events. They will do a great job spearheading this, and you will all have a wonderful time celebrating and appreciating your students.

The following are just a few ideas for signs to post throughout the school:

We love you, students; we think you're great
And to you, this week we dedicate
We thank you for choosing to come to our school
And we want you to know that we think you RULE!

Students have CLASS!

We Love Our Students!

We Appreciate Our Students!

Students, we hope you know that we care.
We think you're the best students anywhere!

Don't be surprised if during Student Appreciation Week you witness any of the following:

- Better student behavior
- Fewer discipline referrals
- Fewer teacher complaints
- Fewer parent complaints
- Happier-looking teachers
- Happier-looking students
- Words or notes of thanks from students
- Words or notes of thanks from parents
- Words or notes of thanks from teachers

Notes

The Ten-Minute Inservice

Dealing with Negative Co-Workers

PURPOSE

Negative Nelly

Negative Nelly teaches at my school
She thinks that being negative is cool
She warns of bad students, bad adults, and bad things
Each day, it's a song of doom that she sings
She's managed to acquire a very small following
Of other naysayers intent on wallowing
In gossip and pettiness and bitterness and complaints
All who will listen, Nelly gladly taints
So do not listen, and do not follow
In anything negative, do not wallow
Just be the most optimistic teacher you know
And down Nelly's path, you'll never go.

You know this teacher. She's on every faculty, and there's just no pleasing her. The students are bad, the parents are bad, the administration is bad, and bashing all of them is good. She is probably a good person, somewhere deep down, but she has developed a very bad habit, one that is actually quite dangerous on any school campus.

Although it's obvious that Negative Nelly (or Nelson) is not very popular with the majority of the faculty (or students or parents), and many tend to avoid her, at all costs, most of your teachers do not realize that they don't have to avoid her at all. Instead, they can use some simple techniques to defuse Nelly and her negative behavior. Today you'll show them how.

INSERVICE

Begin the inservice by sharing the poem about Negative Nelly. Then say, *You may have never yet encountered this type of teacher, but some day you might.* What you've done here is given Nelly an "out." Maybe you're not speaking about her. Maybe you haven't noticed that she leans in a negative direction. Maybe no one else has noticed. Or have they? You see, you've got Nelly thinking. You've got her followers listening. And you've already got the positive teachers silently cheering you on.

Next, ask the following questions:

- Have you ever known a negative person? No names, please. Just get that person in your mind.

- How do you feel around that person?

- How do others feel around that person?

- Have you ever known a negative teacher? Maybe you were taught by a negative teacher when you were in school? Again, no names, please.

- How was that teacher viewed by you and others?

- Did you or others try to avoid that teacher?

- Was that teacher a little intimidating?

- What kind of influence do you think a Negative Nelly (or Nelson) would have on a faculty or on students?

Discuss the fact that most teachers tend to avoid Negative Nelly. Worse yet, some even engage in negative conversations with her. It's not necessarily that they enjoy it, but many don't know what else to do. Tell them that today you'll show them a very productive (and fun) way to stop avoiding her and start removing her fuse. Say, *I'm going to show you all how to strip Nelly (if you should ever meet her) of all her power.*

You may be thinking, "But Negative Nelly will be sitting in this meeting. Once I share the secrets of defusing her, she'll know what the others are doing when they use these techniques on her." Exactly.

Here are a few quick and easy ways for your teachers to remove Nelly's power and to send a message, loudly and clearly, that they won't become her followers:

- The next time Nelly speaks unkindly about a student, simply say, "I love that student." Even if you've never met that student, say, "I love that student." Nelly will have no comeback for that, and you will have made a very powerful, positive statement about how you feel about students.

- For teachers new to the faculty, Nelly is a magnet. She loves warning of the bad students they will be teaching. When she does, there's a trick to defusing her. Simply say, "Thank you so much for telling me about these students. These kinds of students are the reason I became a teacher. You obviously must care a lot about them to have taken time out of your busy schedule to come and speak with me about them. I'm so glad they'll be in my classroom. They obviously need caring teachers such as you and me. I'll keep you posted on their progress."

- If Nelly ever approaches you offering any type of gossip, you can always say, "I'd love to chat, but I'm in a rush. See you later." And then leave. Gossip is hot. She'll quickly feel the need to find another listening ear. But if you're all using this technique, her gossip will never travel!

- When Nelly speaks unkindly about a parent, say, "Whenever I think about the fact that not all parents rear their children as we wish they did, I quickly remind myself of how lucky some students are to spend so many hours with positive people like us at school each day."

IMPLEMENTATION

Tell your teachers that the bottom line is that Nelly continues her negativism because someone is enabling her. Challenge them never to be enablers of negative teachers. Tell them there's just no place for Negative Nelly in a school setting.

Send them off with two tasks: (1) to attempt to use the techniques you just shared if they ever encounter Nelly or one of her followers, and (2) to send you a quick note or stop by to tell you about their successes in using these techniques. Now you've really put the ball in Nelly's court. She's now going to be very careful about saying anything negative about anyone. First, it would be embarrassing to recognize that some of her co-workers are using these techniques on her, and second, she's worried that someone might report her if she does. Nelly is much less powerful already. From enabled to disabled in ten minutes!

Notes

The Ten-Minute Classroom Makeover

PURPOSE

It is difficult to flip through the channels on your television and not happen upon several programs about home, yard, or work space makeovers. Most people like their surroundings to look nice, but many of them need guidance in doing so. If that weren't the case, these makeover programs would quickly die. Instead, they're gaining steam.

Our living and working spaces say a lot to others about who we are as people. When you walk into a teacher's classroom (a teacher of any grade level and any subject area), you can instantly know a lot about that teacher. This is due to the fact that people's physical environments tend to be mirrors of their inner selves.

A disorganized, messy, or cluttered classroom expresses those exact traits in that teacher. A well-organized, cheery, colorful environment expresses those traits in that teacher. Students pick up on these subtleties (or not-so-subtleties), though not usually at a conscious level. We won't delve into any more detail in regard to the psychological meanings behind the environments in which people live and work. Instead, we'll focus on the fact that all students deserve to spend their days in neat, organized, cheerful, welcoming classroom environments.

You don't have to spend lots of money to create a nice, pleasant, welcoming environment. That's good news, as most teachers aren't (financially) wealthy people. Some teachers on your faculty have created beautiful, welcoming environments for their students. Some display traits of hoarding, and we won't go there, figuratively or literally. Others have neat environments, but those environments appear and feel cold and sterile and unfriendly. Other environments are colorful, cheery, and well organized, yet they display only the teacher's personality, as they lack any evidence of student work. Shouldn't all classrooms be a reflection of teachers *and* students? That's the ideal! And that's the kind of classroom you are going to help all your teachers create today. Nothing fancy, nothing expensive, and nothing time-consuming. Well, okay, your hoarders are going to have to spend some time getting rid of all that "stuff." But that purging is long overdue, isn't it?

INSERVICE

Begin your inservice today with the following questions and the discussion they prompt:

- Would you agree that people's physical environments reveal a lot about their personalities?

- Is it true that you can walk into someone's home and learn a lot about that person just by viewing his or her physical surroundings?

- Knowing your students, do you think you could predict, with a high degree of accuracy, what their bedrooms at home look like?

- What do our classrooms say about us, as teachers and as people?

Next, give them the following multiple-choice questions and have them answer as a group:

1. Which environment do you think students would prefer:

   a. One with signs of welcome

   b. One with no signs of welcome

2. Which environment is more conducive to learning?

   a. One that is organized

   b. One that is disorganized

3. Which environment would help students feel a sense of ownership?

   a. One with student work displayed

   b. One with no student work displayed

4. Which environment would feel more welcoming to students?

   a. One that is colorful

   b. One that lacks color

Although the teachers don't know this yet, they have just agreed, by correctly answering the questions on the multiple-choice "quiz" you just gave, that classrooms should be welcoming, should be organized, should display student work, and should be colorful. So now you say, *I agree with all of your answers. I agree that in every classroom in this school, we should see evidence of the following: (1) signs of welcome, (2) basic organization, (3) displays of student work, and (4) color.*

Discuss the fact that people don't have to be "neat freaks" to have well-organized environments. You don't have to have seventeen signs of welcome, either. One sign that says "Welcome to Our Classroom" will suffice—and that sign is free if you allow the students to make it. You don't have to have wall-to-wall student work displayed, but you should always have at least one piece of each student's best work displayed. For some teachers, it's as simple as having a bulletin board titled "Our Best Work." To cover this board, students choose a piece of work they would like to have displayed. And how difficult is it to add a little color to the room? You don't have to paint the room. A plant adds color. Student artwork adds color. Colorful signs add color. And remember, color is not just for elementary classrooms.

IMPLEMENTATION

Now say, *We all agree on the kind of classroom environment our students deserve at school. So now let's make sure we are providing that environment in every classroom. We're going to make this fun by turning it into a contest. We'll all be competing for [name the prize, and make it a good one]. I'll give you all two weeks to get your classrooms ready, though many of you will only need thirty minutes. At the end of two weeks, we will have a drawing for the [prize]. In order to get your name into the drawing, your classroom simply has to have these four elements: (1) at least one sign of welcome, (2) evidence of organization, (3) display of student work, and (4) color.*

At the end of the two-week period, walk through all of the teachers' classrooms looking for those four criteria. Remember that you are *not* looking for perfection. **And this is not a contest for the most beautiful or best-decorated classroom**. The purpose of this activity is simply for everyone to provide students with environments conducive to learning—and this is the quickest, simplest way we know of to get that accomplished. Now put all eligible names into a drawing and proclaim a winner. For those who did not meet the eligibility criteria, a private conference might be in order. Be sure that that conference is held in your well-organized, colorful, welcoming office.

Notes

_____

_____

_____

_____

_____

_____

_____

_____

_____

_____

_____

_____

_____

The Teachers' Lounge

PURPOSE

Ah, the teachers' lounge . . . just the mention of the teachers' lounge can evoke negative emotions from your positive teachers. In fact, the positive teachers often advise new teachers, "Stay away from the teachers' lounge!" The advice is well meant. We used to offer the same advice to new teachers. But we've changed our approach. Now, instead of telling new teachers (and veterans) to avoid the teachers' lounge, we encourage teachers to go to the lounge and make a point of smiling and speaking of positive things. This kind of behavior can have a powerful effect on anyone with a more negative mind-set.

We have helped many teachers turn their schools' teachers' lounges into positive places where teachers can put their feet up and relax for a few minutes each day, enjoying the companionship of other positive co-workers. How have we helped them accomplish this? It's really quite simple. We've encouraged them to

- Stop avoiding the teachers' lounge.
- Enlist the support of a few positive co-workers and frequent the lounge as often as your schedule allows.
- Enter the lounge with a smile on your face.
- Leave the lounge with a smile on your face.
- Speak well of students while you are in the lounge.
- Speak well of the school while you are in the lounge.
- Speak of things that are positive, even if those things don't relate to the school, while in the lounge.

It's true that misery loves company. Miserable people who congregate in one place will attract nothing but other miserable people. The good news is that the reverse is also true. Surely you have more positive than negative teachers on your faculty. And those positive people deserve a break every once in a while. They deserve to have a place where they can go to get a cup of coffee and relax, even if it's only for six minutes and seventeen seconds. And you are about to endear yourself to your positive teachers by conducting this inservice.

INSERVICE

Begin by asking your teachers to fill in the blank:

New teachers almost always receive the following advice when they begin teaching: "If there is one place in the school you will want to avoid, it's the _____."

Your teachers will know the answer, so don't be concerned that you may have to fill in the blank for them. After they answer, ask, *Why are so many teachers warned, in any school, to stay away from the teachers' lounge?* Allow for a few minutes of discussion. During the discussion, ask a few sobering questions:

- Is it ever appropriate to gossip about others?
- Can we ever help students by speaking negatively of them?

- Can we ever help adults by speaking negatively of them?

- Didn't we all enter this profession to help people?

- Why do you think there are teachers out there (though we hope not on this faculty) who would ever even entertain the thought of speaking ill of students or their parents?

Ask any other questions you'd like. The point is to get everyone—especially your lounge gossips (and yes, they exist in every school)—thinking about the negative consequences of their negative actions. This isn't about only the lounge, of course. It just so happens that the lounge is often a place where negative people love to congregate.

Next, assume ignorance by saying, *I'm sure that people are not speaking negatively of others in our own lounge. But let's all work hard at making the atmosphere in our lounge (and in our school) even more positive than it already is. How do you think we could help accomplish that?* By asking this question, you are helping them take ownership of making the lounge a pleasant place to take a break.

At this point, designate someone to document the ideas (possibly on chart paper) that teachers offer for making the lounge more positive. And remember that you can lead them, through your questioning, to the best possible answers. For instance, if you really want the list to include the idea that while visiting the lounge, teachers could share positive things that are going on in their classrooms, then lead them there with your questioning. Here's the question: *Do you think it might be helpful to share positive things that are happening in your classrooms while you are visiting with one another in the lounge?* They are going to agree. Then say, *Great. Then let's add that to the list.* You get the idea.

IMPLEMENTATION

Send your teachers away today by encouraging them to make the teachers' lounge the most positive place on the campus. Tell them you'll do your best to help them accomplish that. Say, *You can expect to see me smiling as I pass through the lounge also!*

In order to realize the benefits of a more positive atmosphere in the teachers' lounge, you are going to have to enlist the support of some of your most positive teachers. Treat it like an experiment. Tell them you need their help in changing the overall atmosphere in the lounge, and you're hoping you can count on their assistance. Even if they just occasionally walk through the lounge with smiles and positive comments, it will have a positive impact. Go into the lounge yourself, and be all smiles.

This experiment can actually be quite fun. The key is to make the lounge such a positive place that it makes the negative teachers uncomfortable to be there or, better yet, brings the negative teachers around to a more positive way of thinking and behaving. Either way, you can't lose.

Notes

Positive Communication with *All* Parents

PURPOSE

Is it realistic to assume that there will come a day when, through your tireless efforts, you will finally get all parents to come to school for conferences, volunteer to help with fundraisers, serve on parent committees, and participate actively in their children's schooling? Of course not. But is it worth the effort to take steps to ensure that all parents receive positive communication from their children's teachers on a regular basis, even if they're not active participants in their children's schooling? Absolutely. Is it realistic to believe that when parents enjoy a positive relationship with their children's teachers, they might be more likely to answer the phone when receiving a call from the school or to respond to a teacher who sends a note home or requests a conference? Definitely.

In today's inservice, you will be sharing a strategy for opening the lines of communication between teachers and parents.

INSERVICE

Ask your teachers if they agree that parental involvement is important. They will, of course. Ask them if they would like to see increased parental involvement. Ask if they'd like to enjoy even better relationships with their students' parents than they currently do. Discuss the fact that although we, as educators, cannot force parents to become more involved in their children's education, we can certainly take simple steps to open the lines of communication with them.

Tell your teachers that there are endless ways to communicate positively with parents, but today you'll be focusing on just one. The idea is simple, quick, and easy to do. It will require less than a minute a day on the part of your teachers, and it has the potential to have a very positive impact on the relationships between teachers and parents.

Show this sample note to your teachers.

Dear Ms. Brooks:

I am so proud of Daniel. Today in class, he worked really hard and completed all of his work. I'm happy to share this good news with you.

Ms. Carter

Next, show your teachers a blank note, such as the one here, that only requires them to fill in the blanks. Point out that writing such a note to send home to a parent should take less than a minute.

Dear _____:

I am so proud of _____ because

_____

_____

_____

I'm happy to share this good news with you.

_____

You and your faculty might decide to use our sample or to write your own version of a positive note to parents. You might choose to include the school's logo or add some type of graphic design. When you finalize how the note will look, type several onto one page. This page can then be photocopied or put into an electronic file so that each teacher has ready-to-go notes at hand. In other words, do the work for them so that they don't view this as a chore or yet more paperwork.

The object is to have each teacher send one note home per class each day. Writing the note should take each teacher about thirty seconds. The note is prewritten. The teachers simply have to fill in the blanks.

Let teachers know that they are not at all limited to sending only one note home per day. Give them the following example:

Let's say you are a teacher who is sending one note home a day. You already gave Jordan a note to bring to his mother, telling her of something he did particularly well today in class. Lydia is a student in your class who displays a lot of inappropriate behavior. You have been trying to find an opportunity to send a positive note home to her parents, but, to the best of your knowledge, that opportunity has not yet presented itself. You suddenly notice that she just got busy on her assignment. Normally, it takes much effort on your part to help her get started on assignments, but today, she did it on her own. Hurry and write that note. It doesn't matter that you already sent your allotted one note home for the day. It's worth the thirty seconds to write yet another note—this one to Lydia's parents—telling them how proud you are of Lydia for getting to work so quickly today.

Share a few examples of the types of behaviors that might be included in positive notes to parents:

- Good behavior

- Improved behavior

- Accomplishment of a certain skill

- Improvement in schoolwork

- Improvement in work habits

- Improvement in organizational skills

- A good deed of any kind

- The fact that the student helped another student in some way

- The fact that the student helped you in some way

- An award that the student won

- A contest that the student won

Add a few of your own examples here. You might even ask your teachers to come up with a few ideas.

- _____

- _____

- _____

- _____

- _____

IMPLEMENTATION

Have each teacher send one note home per class each day. If a teacher chooses to send more, that's fine. But you're only asking each to send one. The object is to ensure that every parent receives at least one positive comment about his or her child at least once a month or so. This way, you are guaranteeing that each parent will receive several positive notes from each teacher about his or her child during the school year. That's several more than some parents have ever received about their children.

On those occasions when the teacher has to contact a parent regarding something of a more serious nature regarding his child, that parent may be more apt to work cooperatively with the teacher if he has already been receiving positive notes. If all he ever receives are negative notes of communication, the teacher may very likely meet with a more defensive attitude.

There is no downside to this type of activity. Parents welcome positive notes from teachers. It makes them feel proud of their children and proud of themselves.

It also promotes a more positive relationship between them and their children's teachers. It may even foster more positive relationships between parents and their children. It helps students feel pride in themselves. (Students love delivering these types of notes to their parents.) It serves to promote more positive relationships between teachers and students. And it also helps your teachers begin focusing on the many positive actions of all their students.

One little note can make a very big difference.

Notes

_____
_____
_____
_____
_____
_____
_____
_____
_____
_____
_____
_____
_____
_____
_____
_____
_____
_____
_____
_____
_____

PART 4

Learning from Others

Teacher Report Cards, Part 1

PURPOSE

Every few weeks or months, in just about every school, every student receives a report card. Although often dreaded, these documents give important information about how each student is performing academically, socially, and behaviorally. Yet when do the students have the opportunity to report on how their teachers are performing? Sure, the principal reports, through a few observations, on each teacher's performance. But who better to tell teachers about how well (or not so well) they are doing on a daily basis than the teachers' own clients? If you really want to know how a teacher is doing, ask the students! How? By allowing them to fill out teacher report cards.

Now before you think, "Oh, no! My teachers will go ballistic if I add yet another evaluation tool to their plates," let us explain. The teacher report card is an informal means for students to provide feedback to their teachers. These report cards have nothing to do with a teacher's performance scores. But they have a whole *lot* to do with improving teacher performance. We'll tell you exactly how to introduce the concept to your teachers, but first we'll explain both what a teacher report card is and what it can serve to accomplish.

A teacher report card is a simple, informal evaluation completed by students each time they receive their own report cards. These documents have no space for student names, because the best way to get honest feedback from students is to allow them to express themselves anonymously. Sample questions include the following:

Sample Teacher Report Card

Does my teacher care about me as a person?

Does my teacher hold me accountable for my actions?

Does my teacher do his/her best to make class interesting?

Does my teacher help me when I am struggling?

Is this class interesting? If not, what could my teacher do to make this class more interesting?

Does my teacher allow me to actively participate in lessons?

Does my teacher treat me with respect?

Do I feel successful in this class? If not, what could my teacher do to help me become more successful?

Does my teacher enjoy teaching?

Is my teacher a good role model for me?

One thing I really like about this class is _____.

One thing I do not like about this class is _____.

If I could change one thing about this class, it would be _____.

Now that you have an idea of what a teacher report card actually looks like, can you see the possibilities? When students are afforded the opportunity to grade the performance of their teachers, several things are accomplished:

- The process holds teachers accountable for their actions, because they know they will be "graded" by their students.

- It provides valuable feedback to teachers about their performance in the classroom. How the students view their teachers *does* matter.

- It provides students with a sense of ownership in the classroom.

- It tells students that their input is valued.

- It keeps teachers on their toes, which is where they should always be.

We know of many schools and teachers who use teacher report cards with great success. Not surprisingly, students love the idea. It gives them a sense of worth and importance, knowing that their opinions matter to their teachers. One teacher shared the following story with us. Feel free to share it with your teachers after you discuss the new teacher report card idea:

> On the first day of school, I tell my students that just as I will be grading them, they will also be grading me. I say, "I want to get straight A's, but you can't give me those unless I earn them. Therefore, I'll tell you what's going to be on the teacher report card in advance, so that you'll know what to look for prior to grading me. I also want you to know that you will not be putting your names on these report cards. I want your honest feedback."
>
> I then give each a copy of the report card. I say things like, "One of the items on the report card asks if I, as your teacher, hold you accountable for your actions. And I want an A, so I'm going to hold you accountable for your actions. But notice it also asks if I treat you with dignity. I promise to do that also. So even if you do something wrong and I have to hold you accountable for it, I promise to treat you with respect and dignity." I do this with every item on the report card. There are no secrets. We all know, in advance, what they can and should expect from me.
>
> The same week that they get their report cards, I also get mine. I put a student in charge of handing these out. The students complete the report cards, anonymously, and then the assigned student puts them all into an envelope and puts them on my desk. I read through them carefully, and I take notes. The following day, I hold a class discussion and discuss the results. I don't, of course, discuss every comment from every report card, but I do address patterns.

For instance, if several students suggest that they would like to work in groups more often, I say something like, "Several of you mentioned that you would like to work in groups more often. I think that's a great idea, so we'll start doing more of that." I have to say that these report cards have helped me to have a better grasp on how my students perceive me as a teacher. They have provided me with some excellent ideas for new and different ways to teach the same old concepts, and I'm definitely a better teacher because of it.

As an aside, before you conduct this particular inservice, run the idea of a teacher report card by your star teachers and then be prepared to be smothered with hugs. (You may want to wear your shin guards when you run the idea by your least effective teachers.)

INSERVICE

At today's inservice, you will simply be introducing the concept of a teacher report card to your teachers. Begin by asking the following questions:

- Would you agree that because none of us ever completely master the art of teaching, we are all striving to become better teachers?

- Would you agree that our students are our clients and that they are the reasons we are teachers?

- Would you also agree that we, in education, rarely allow our clients to tell us how we're performing? Why do you think that's so?

After a brief discussion of these questions, say, *I've already run this new idea by a few teachers* [don't name anyone, of course], *and I'm happy to say that they were as excited about it as I am. So I'm eager to share with you the idea of implementing simple, informal teacher report cards. I'll tell you more about this in a minute, but know, in advance, that these are very informal, and they will be for your eyes only.*

Next, tell them what a teacher report card is, what it looks like, and what the benefits of implementing a teacher report card will be. Conduct the entire inservice in a very positive manner. You are operating under the assumptions that they *all* want to improve and that they will all be excited about this new idea. Will they all be excited? No. But your least excited teachers will be the ones most in need of such an instrument.

IMPLEMENTATION

Assign a small group of teachers, consisting of a few excellent teachers and a few less-than-excellent teachers, to be in charge of collecting ideas for a schoolwide teacher report card. Tell all teachers to send any suggestions they may have to this group of teachers before the next inservice. You want them all to take ownership of this project, so include teachers at all levels of effectiveness. Treat them all as if they're excellent teachers with nothing to fear, and send them off to create the new report card.

Notes

_____
_____
_____
_____
_____
_____
_____
_____
_____
_____
_____
_____
_____
_____
_____
_____
_____
_____

Teacher Report Cards, Part 2

PURPOSE

In the previous inservice, you introduced the concept of teacher report cards. We're guessing that some of your teachers were happy about this and others were not. You, of course, are acting as though you believe that everyone is as excited about the new report cards as you are.

At the end of the last inservice, you asked a small committee to gather feedback and suggestions for the new report card. You, of course, have a say as to what goes into the final document that will become the new schoolwide teacher report card. If there is something you feel needs to be on that report card and it is not included in the committee's suggestions, simply add it.

As a reminder, here again is a sample teacher report card:

- Does my teacher care about me as a person?

- Does my teacher hold me accountable for my actions?

- Does my teacher do his/her best to make class interesting?

- Does my teacher help me when I am struggling?

- Is this class interesting? If not, what could my teacher do to make this class more interesting?

- Does my teacher allow me to actively participate in lessons?

- Does my teacher treat me with respect?

- Do I feel successful in this class? If not, what could my teacher do to help me become more successful?

- Does my teacher enjoy teaching?

- Is my teacher a good role model for me?

- One thing I really like about this class is _____.

- One thing I do not like about this class is _____.

- If I could change one thing about this class, it would be

  _____.

INSERVICE

Once again, share your excitement about the new teacher report cards with the faculty. Then have someone from the committee share the suggestions they received. At this point, you have two options:

Option 1: Have someone read all of the suggested items and then have the teachers, as a group, narrow those down to no more than fifteen items. Note that if your school has a large variety of grade levels, the report cards might look a little different for the students in lower grades than those of the students in upper grades. Tell the teachers that you will have these suggestions incorporated into the new schoolwide teacher report card and that they'll receive a copy within the next week.

Option 2: If you want a little more control over what goes into the final document, you might simply choose, at this time, to collect the ideas from the committee and tell them that you will consider all of them when finalizing the document. However, if you have a couple of outstanding teachers on your committee, you can usually choose option 1, trusting them to come up with an excellent document. It's your call.

IMPLEMENTATION

The implementation phase will be ongoing. Every time students get their report cards, the teachers will also be receiving report cards from the students. And teachers will need to be reminded of this on an ongoing basis because, for some, it will be quite convenient to "forget."

Again, these teacher report cards are valuable tools for fostering both teacher growth and better relationships between teachers and students.

Before you send your teachers away today, remind them that

- These report cards are informal.
- No one will see these but you, the teacher.
- It is important that student anonymity is maintained so that they feel safe in expressing their opinions.
- These report cards will send a message to students that you want to be the best teacher you can be.
- You will be sending a message to students that you value their input.
- Don't be surprised at an occasional inappropriate comment from a student.
- No matter what, do not let the students know that any comment has upset you in any way.
- When you meet with your students to address some of their concerns, comments, and suggestions, say, "In the interest of saving time, I've combined lots of the comments and suggestions." This way, you never even mention a comment that was in any way inappropriate.
- Be sure to end your discussion by thanking the students for their honest and useful feedback. Tell them it means a lot to you.

Notes

Administrator Report Card

PURPOSE

In the previous two inservices, you have helped your teachers develop a teacher report card that will give students the opportunity to provide useful feedback to their teachers. If you really want your teachers to accept and embrace this concept, why not treat them as your own students and allow them to fill out an administrator report card for you? A scary concept, isn't it? That's exactly how some of your teachers are feeling about having their students evaluate them. Unless it's sugarcoated, the truth about how people perceive us and what they feel about the job we are doing isn't always sweet. But that truth can serve as a springboard for self-improvement. Just as no teacher ever completely masters the art of teaching, no administrator or staff developer ever masters the art of leading.

Your report card should look as much like the teacher report card as possible. Here's an example:

Sample Administrator Report Card

Does my administrator care about me as a person?

Does my administrator hold me accountable for my actions?

Does my administrator do his/her best to make this school the best it can be?

Does my administrator help me when I am struggling?

Following an observation, does my administrator provide me with honest feedback and constructive criticism?

Does my administrator allow me to actively participate in school activities?

Does my administrator encourage me to become involved with committee work?

Does my administrator treat me with respect?

Do I feel successful as a teacher in this school? If not, what could my administrator do to help me become more successful?

Does my administrator appear to enjoy his/her job?

Is my administrator a good role model for me?

One thing I really like about this school is _____.

One thing I really like about my administrator is _____.

One thing I do not like about this school is _____.

One thing I do not like about my administrator is _____.

If I could change one thing about this school, it would be

_____.

If I could change one thing about my administrator, it would be _____.

[Note: If you are a staff development person or a teacher leader, simply modify the report card so that the questions apply to you and your particular roles and responsibilities with teachers.]

INSERVICE

Here's a sample script for conducting this inservice:

I'm really pleased with the teacher report card that you have all helped develop, and I firmly believe that your students' honest feedback about your performance will help you become even better teachers than you already are.

I do realize that allowing your students to "grade" you can be a little scary. But we all know that students will tell you how they really feel, not just what they think you want to hear.

I want you to know that I am not asking anything of you that I'm not willing to do myself. So today I would like you, my "students," to fill out a report card on my performance. Just like the report card that you gave your students, this will be done anonymously. I truly want your honest feedback. And yes, I'm a little scared to receive it!

By giving your teachers the opportunity to evaluate you, you will accomplish a great deal:

- You will earn their respect.
- You will send the message that their opinions matter.
- You will show your willingness to address their issues and concerns and consider their suggestions.
- You will endear yourself to them by showing them that you don't ask them to do things you aren't willing to do yourself.

Now hand out the administrator report cards to your teachers, leave the room, and ask the teachers to leave the cards in a designated box or envelope on their way out.

IMPLEMENTATION

Just as you have asked your teachers to read their students' report cards carefully, spend some time reading the results of your administrator report cards. Give some thought to how you will address positive comments, negative comments, and teacher suggestions. Then sit with your teachers and address those comments. Be honest about your response to the report card results, and talk about what you are willing and able to change as a result of their suggestions. If you were upset or hurt by any of the negative comments (and yes, there will always be a few), be careful not to reveal those emotions in your discussion with your teachers. Instead, you might say something to this effect: *Even though not all of the comments were positive, I respect the fact that you were willing to share your true feelings. Please know that I am working, every day, at being the best leader I can be, for you and for our students. I do realize that not all of my decisions are popular, but I can assure you that I make each of them based on what I believe at the time to be in the best interest of our students.*

Never end the discussion with the negative comments, however. Address those somewhere in the middle of your discussion and don't dwell on them. Begin and end your discussion on a high note.

Notes

_____
_____
_____
_____
_____
_____
_____
_____
_____
_____
_____
_____
_____
_____
_____
_____
_____
_____
_____
_____
_____
_____
_____

What's Working for Others

PURPOSE

Too often, teachers teach in isolation and don't have much contact with their co-workers. They're busy teaching their own students in their own classrooms, so there's not a lot of time for collaboration. That's regrettable, because teachers can learn so much from one another. When teachers do get together, be it in the lounge or during a planning period, oftentimes gripe sessions ensue, and very little that's productive is accomplished.

A teacher shared the following with us:

> I teach with so many wonderful teachers, but we rarely have time to collaborate and share our ideas with one another. One day, some of the teachers were discussing the fact that we really could learn a lot from one another if we only had the time to do it. Our principal

overheard the conversation and said, "You're right. Let's make time for doing that." He called a meeting of the faculty and asked each of us to bring one idea or story about something that was working really well for us in our classrooms. The topic was student behavior. The only rule for the session was that no one would be allowed to complain about students or student behavior. Instead, we were to share techniques that were working well when dealing with behavior issues. We all sat around and shared our successes. One teacher had the task of recording the ideas and then putting them into a document to share with everyone.

That one meeting was more productive than any meeting we had ever had. Many of the teachers were amazed at how much there was to learn from people they work with on a daily basis. One of the keys to the success of this sharing session, of course, was the structure. Each had a turn to share one idea, and no one was allowed to gripe. I hate to admit that it was the first time (and I've been teaching a long time) that I've ever been a part of such a positive, productive sharing session. Since then, we have decided to hold these sharing sessions monthly. The topics include behavior issues, instructional strategies, getting parents involved, etc. I believe we can all learn from one another, and I have to say that I have really filled my bag of tricks with many of the suggestions from my co-workers. It also makes me feel really good when one of my co-workers says, "I'm using the technique you shared last week, and it's really working great. Thanks!"

For this inservice, you will be bringing all your teachers together to share suggestions and stories about what is working well for them in their classrooms. You've got a wealth of information right there on your own faculty. Why not afford everyone the opportunity to tap into this valuable resource?

Prior to this inservice,

- Ask each teacher to bring in one classroom management strategy that is working well and to be prepared to share this strategy with the faculty.

- Designate someone to lead the discussion. After you do your small part in introducing the sharing session, you may want to leave. The session will practically run itself, but it is a good idea to have a teacher assigned to facilitate the discussion.

- Designate someone to put together a document listing each teacher's strategy. (This should be distributed to all teachers within no more than a week of the inservice.)

INSERVICE

Please note that as the administrator or staff developer, you will complete your portion of this inservice in ten minutes or less, but the teachers should be allowed to stay as long as they'd like in order to discuss ideas with one another.

Begin the inservice by sharing the teacher's story that we just shared with you. Next, share a few successful classroom management strategies you've recently observed. Here are a few examples:

- I was walking down the hall the other day, and a student was running. I noticed that Ms. Barker calmly said, "Thanks, Matt, for remembering that we have to walk in the hallways." Matt immediately stopped running. It was such a positive approach, and it worked beautifully! She didn't dare him to do it again. She didn't appear angry or frustrated. Instead, she thanked him for remembering that he shouldn't be doing what he was doing. Perfect.

- While I was observing in Mr. P's class, a student took out his cell phone and began texting. Mr. P walked up to the student and whispered something to him, and the student put the cell phone away. Because he whispered to the student, I had no idea what he said, but I was surely curious to know. After the observation, I asked Mr. P what he had said to the student. Mr. P told me, "Oh, I just asked him a question. I asked him if he thought he could remember to keep the cell phone in his desk. I told him if he thought he might have trouble remembering, I would be happy to hold it for him until the end of class. He chose to keep the cell phone in his desk." There was no power struggle. Mr. P simply acted as though he was providing a kind reminder and even being kind enough to offer to hold the phone for the student if need be. It worked!

- In Ms. Tanner's class last week, a student was off task. Ms. Tanner, who is always walking around the room as she teaches, passed that student's desk and tapped him twice on the shoulder. She didn't stop next to his desk. She just tapped him as she passed his desk. I asked her about it after class, and she told me that all the students know the signal for getting back on task. If a student is off task, she passes his or her desk and lightly taps twice on the student's shoulder. There's no discussion. There's no embarrassment. It's just a friendly way for her to remind the student to get back on task.

Add some of your own ideas here.

- _____
  _____
  _____
  _____
  _____

- _____
  _____
  _____
  _____
  _____

- _____
  _____
  _____
  _____
  _____

You might choose to lead the sharing session yourself or have a teacher facilitate it. It is likely that not all of the teachers will have the opportunity to share their techniques aloud, but all of their techniques will go into one document that will be shared with everyone. You have already given someone the task of compiling this document. A good idea is to have everyone email strategies to this person. Then, with a little cutting and pasting, all the ideas can easily be compiled into one document and emailed to you and all the teachers.

IMPLEMENTATION

For the assignment, have teachers return to their classrooms to try at least one strategy they have learned from today's session. We feel certain that after realizing the benefit of such a sharing session, you'll soon begin scheduling even more of these. You don't have to facilitate these types of sessions. Instead, assign a different teacher each time to be the facilitator. You may also want to schedule grade-level or subject-area sharing sessions.

Again, the key to the success of these sharing sessions lies in their structure. Gripe sessions are to be conducted elsewhere, because there is no place for griping in positive sharing sessions.

Notes

_____
_____
_____
_____
_____
_____
_____
_____
_____
_____
_____
_____
_____

Teachers Observing Teachers

PURPOSE

When asked how often they observe their co-workers teaching, most teachers will say that such an opportunity is either rare or nonexistent. When asked why, many administrators will say either that they haven't given it much consideration or, if they have, that it presents a scheduling nightmare. Who will watch Teacher A's class when she goes to observe Teacher B? How quickly we forget that teachers are creative and resourceful people!

We know of a principal who decided that she wanted to provide her teachers with the opportunity to observe one other. Here's how she described it to us:

> I've got a wonderful faculty and a wonderful school overall. On that wonderful faculty, however, I've got a few not-so-wonderful teachers. I believe all of them are quite capable of being wonderful, and it's my

job as their leader to help them to realize that. Even my best teachers will admit that they are always looking for new ideas to improve their skills. I decided that one of the best ways to help all of my teachers to improve their skills was to allow them to begin learning from one another by observing each other in the classrooms. The experience has been nothing short of amazing!

Here's how we do it: Once a month, each teacher observes one other teacher for a minimum of thirty minutes. If several teachers want to observe one teacher at the same time, that's fine. It's not unusual to walk into Teacher C's room and see Teachers A, D, and G sitting in the back of the room observing. That's because Teacher C is skilled at incorporating technology, and the three teachers observing not only want to see this in action but all have planning periods at that particular time. We give the teachers the responsibility of setting up the monthly schedules by simply providing them with sign-up sheets. Each teacher has to sign up for one class period a week where others may feel free to come in and observe. The teachers decide on a category of strength—classroom management, student engagement, technology, cooperative grouping, instructional strategies, etc. The categories can change from month to month. Under each teacher's name, there are six slots. That means that no more than six co-workers will observe each teacher each month.

To give you an example, Teacher A signs her name under the category of classroom management and designates Monday at second period as her available time to be observed by others. (The structure of the sign-up sheet ensures that there are teachers who are available to be observed at all class periods, because the teachers only go out to observe others during their planning periods.) This month, maybe three people will come to observe Teacher A. She knows, in advance, that Teacher Y will observe her this Monday and Teachers G and S will observe her next Monday. She will have no other observations by co-workers for the rest of the month. But she knows this in advance, so there are no "surprise observations" by co-workers. Teacher A also has to observe one teacher this month. She decides she wants to see someone using cooperative grouping, so she chooses one of the teachers (who is available to be observed during Teacher A's planning period) on the cooperative grouping list and puts her name into that slot. So now she knows that she will observe Teacher E next Wednesday at fourth period. If it sounds confusing, it's actually not. At the beginning of the month, the teachers know that the sign-up sheets will be on the table in the lounge on a certain day. They actually rush in to try to get preferred time slots and specific teachers to observe. (They also can't wait to see who has signed up to observe THEM.)

As an administrator, I occasionally recommend that certain teachers sign up to be observed in particular areas. For instance, I encourage my strongest classroom managers to put their names on that particular list, because I want as many people as possible to see them in action. I also occasionally tell Teacher J (who is weak in the technology area) that I'd like him to observe someone on that particular list this week. We even have a list titled "Just Plain Good Teaching." In other words, people who are observing a teacher on that list are not looking for anything in particular. They just want to see good teaching in action.

When I first introduced this idea to my faculty, there was a good bit of rumbling. That was only because this concept was so foreign to them. Once they got the hang of it and realized all there was to learn from one another, they loved it. Okay, so my weakest teachers have not all gotten around to the "loving it" stage, but that's fine with me. They're better teachers than they were before we began doing this. ALL of my teachers are better for it. And that was my goal.

Don't we all have the goal of helping every one of our teachers become better than they already are? Can you see the benefits of allowing your teachers to observe each other? Here are just a few of those benefits, though we feel certain you will be able to add to this list:

- Everyone gets observed by co-workers, so they all work really hard at doing their best.

- Your weakest teachers can now learn from your strongest teachers.

- Your strongest teachers, even if observing weaker teachers, always pick up new ideas. If nothing else, your strongest teachers finally realize just how good they themselves are. What a great way to validate them!

- Your teachers work out the schedule with the help of a few sign-up sheets. You don't have any scheduling nightmares.

- All teachers are experiencing ongoing staff development by learning from one another.

INSERVICE

Introduce this concept to your teachers. You might want to share a time in your own career when you benefited from peer observations. Have a few simple sign-up sheets ready to go. Make a big deal out of it, acting as though you assume they will all be as excited as you are to do this. Act as though you are doing a favor for them. In essence, you are, though some of them certainly won't realize this yet. Make it a point to tell them that you are only asking that they observe for thirty minutes a month, during one of their planning periods. If they are absent on observation day, it will be their responsibility to reschedule. As far as having people come in and observe them, well, they'll already be teaching anyway, so you're just asking them to keep on doing what they were already planning to do—no extra work entailed.

IMPLEMENTATION

For the first month, let your teachers sign up to observe whomever they'd like. Don't make any suggestions as to who should be observing whom. You'll want to let them get their feet wet and become comfortable with the idea of both observing their co-workers and being observed by their co-workers. Keep a copy of the sign-up sheets in your office so that you will always know who is observing whom on any given day and at any given class period. If you notice that Teacher B is observing Teacher C today, you might make it a point to seek out either or both of them after the observation and ask how it went.

We suspect you may find this the single most important thing you do this year. You're helping your teachers help one another improve.

Notes

_____
_____
_____
_____
_____
_____
_____
_____
_____
_____
_____
_____
_____
_____
_____
_____
_____
_____
_____
_____
_____
_____
_____
_____
_____
_____
_____
_____
_____
_____
_____
_____
_____
_____

PART 5

What Makes a Great Teacher?

Making Student-Based Decisions

PURPOSE

We're all in this business of education for one reason: the students. So it stands to reason that every decision we make ought to center around one question: Is this best for our students? We believe that if that question were truly at the forefront of every decision made in education, our education system would look a lot different than it does today. So what happened? What else is driving our decisions? Because we're human, sometimes we forget about what's best for the students, and we make decisions based on what's best or easiest for us. Consider the fact that many teachers plan tests that span an entire class period. Are they basing that decision on sound research showing that a fifty-minute test is more effective than one that takes only twenty minutes? Or are they basing that decision on the fact that if the test lasts the whole class period, it's one less lesson plan to write and one much-desired fifty-minute break for them? We've all done this at one time or another, making a decision based on what's best or easiest for us as opposed to what will most help our students. Sometimes we don't even realize what we're doing. For instance, many teachers make their tests last an entire class period simply because that's the way it's always been done, so they assume it must be correct.

Whatever the reason, the fact remains that your teachers don't always make decisions based on what's best for their students. Today's inservice will serve two purposes: (1) to make them aware of what they're basing their decisions on and (2) to help them shift their focus back to the students.

INSERVICE

Begin by sharing the following scenario.

A child begs his parent for permission to stay up one hour later than his typical bedtime. The parent refuses because the child has school in the morning. The child begs louder. The parent remains insistent. The child whines and pleads. Finally, the parent gives in.

Ask, *Have you ever witnessed something like this? Have you ever done something like this? Why do you think the parent eventually gave in? The parent gave in because it was easier to say yes than to endure listening to yet more begging from the child. Initially, the parent made a decision based on what he thought was best for the child. The child didn't see it that way, of course. And eventually the child wore the parent down. When it became too stressful for the parent to deal with the child anymore, the parent took the easy way out. Let's be clear that the parent did not suddenly have a change of heart and realize that his first decision to say no was inappropriate. Instead, he simply decided to do what was easiest as opposed to what he felt was best for his child.*

Remind your teachers that we're all human and that sometimes we substitute what's best for what's easiest when making decisions. We do this as parents, and we do it as educators.

Now give your teachers the following examples and let them decide which options are better for the students, as opposed to those that are easier for the teacher:

> **Scenario:** A teacher finishes her lesson eight minutes before the dismissal bell. Which option is better for students?

a. She tells the students, "If you can find a way to keep yourselves busy and quiet until the bell rings, I won't give you anything else to do."

b. She immediately begins teaching something else, knowing that every minute with a student is an opportunity for learning.

Scenario: A teacher is creating a test, deciding what kinds of items to include. Which option is better for students?

a. A test that consists of all objective answers and can be graded quickly.

b. A test that requires students to discuss, explain, analyze, demonstrate, and so on.

Scenario: A teacher is beginning a new lesson. There is a list of ten vocabulary words provided in the textbook. Which option is better for students?

a. They must use dictionaries to find the word meanings, copying those definitions into their notebooks. Then they have to write a sentence with each word.

b. They discuss each word as a group, figuring out word meanings using context clues, word parts, and so on, and then create group definitions that go up on the wall (and possibly into their notebooks also). Then the students are asked to use the words in spoken sentences. This is a whole-class activity.

Scenario: It's Friday. The teacher is tired. The students are working at computer stations trying to learn a new concept. The teacher has one set of test papers left to grade. Which option is better for students?

a. The teacher lets the students work independently while he sits at his desk and grades the papers.

b. He walks around to each station asking questions, monitoring for understanding, and providing assistance.

Scenario: The class is beginning a new chapter on World War II. Which option is better for students?

a. The teacher tells them to read the chapter and then answer the questions at the end of the chapter.

b. The teacher begins the lesson by allowing students to share their prior knowledge of the war and then has them use the chapter and the Internet (as they work in groups) to find specific information based on questions provided by the teacher. Each group then shares its findings during a class discussion.

Add a few of your own scenarios here.

_____

_____

_____

_____

_____

_____

_____

_____

_____

_____

_____

IMPLEMENTATION

Again, remind your teachers to base *all* decisions on what's best for students, no matter how tempting it may be to base decisions on other factors. Tell them that you are working hard at doing the same. Confide that you struggle at times when you are considering making a change in a program or a change in teaching schedules or when you are deciding how to discipline a student. Remind them that although it would be more "popular" for you to base your decisions on what might be easiest for the teachers, you have to base your decisions on what will benefit the students. You are simply asking them to do the same.

Notes

Because I Like You

PURPOSE

Have you ever asked someone for a favor and been told, "I'll do it, but only because I like you"? That statement, "I'll do it because I like you," holds a profound clue for educators—a clue that is often overlooked. It has been proven, time and again, that people will work harder for those they like; they will buy more from those they like; and they will be more tolerant of the shortcomings of those they like. In short, they will do almost anything for those they like. Yet chances are good that there are teachers on your faculty who've been overheard saying, "Teaching is not a popularity contest. I don't care if the students like me as long as they learn from me." We *know* you've heard it—we've all heard it. The sad fact is that the people saying this are sorely mistaken and misguided. Teaching is most definitely a popularity contest. If the students don't like you, then it's quite likely they won't learn from you. That's why the relationships that teachers establish with their students, good or bad, affect the amount of learning that occurs.

INSERVICE

Begin the inservice by reading, verbatim, the previous paragraph to your teachers. After reading that paragraph, you'll have everyone's attention, guaranteed. Now go over the paragraph, point by point, allowing for discussion following each.

- Have you ever been told, "I'll do it, but only because I like you"?

- In your own schooling, didn't you, as a student, work harder for the teachers you liked?

- If your friend is selling Tupperware, even if you don't need any more Tupperware, won't you be likely to buy yet another piece of something you don't in fact need, just because the person selling it is someone you really like?

- Isn't it true that we are all more tolerant of the shortcomings of the people we like?

- Don't we all have one or two trusted friends who would do almost anything for us because they like us?

- Have you ever overheard a teacher (no names, please) saying, "I don't care if the students like me as long as they learn from me"? Do you realize how very flawed that way of thinking is?

- How important is it to establish positive relationships with the students you teach?

- Why do effective salespeople make "small talk" and try to connect with you on a personal level before asking for the sale?

- How do great coaches succeed in getting average athletes to perform above-average feats?

- Why is it that some teachers can get almost any student to do just about anything?

IMPLEMENTATION

Remind your teachers that teaching *is* a popularity contest. For them to get the most from their students, they have to be seen as likable by their students. Send your teachers back to their classrooms with the task of becoming more likable to their students. If some teachers are at a loss for ways to become more likable, provide them with the following:

Tips for Improving Your Relationships with Students

- Smile often.
- Get to know your students.
- Express belief in your students.
- Be encouraging.
- Be understanding.
- Be compassionate.
- Be the most pleasant person you know.
- Be the most positive person you know.
- Provide assistance to struggling students.
- Teach with gusto.
- Be nice!

Notes

_____
_____
_____
_____
_____
_____
_____
_____
_____
_____
_____
_____

Professionalism Is
as Professionalism Does

PURPOSE

We recently had a conversation with a disgruntled teacher that went like this:

She said, "We aren't respected in this profession. And we aren't respected in this school. The principal is an [expletive], and he's incompetent. The parents don't care. They just let these kids do whatever they want. The students are rude and disrespectful. On top of that, they're lazy. People don't realize how difficult this job is. We're supposed to take a bunch of lazy kids and turn them into productive citizens. I don't get paid enough to put up with this!"

When we asked why she thought the principal was incompetent, she told us that he had the audacity to tell her that she needed to improve her attitude and her teaching skills. Didn't the brief encounter we just shared already hint at the fact that the principal was on target? Through her own words, she announced that she doesn't act in a professional manner, believes she is a victim, is quick to speak negatively of others, labels students as lazy, labels parents as uncaring, and is not happy in her chosen profession.

Because we pride ourselves on being true professionals, we did not ask this question to the teacher: How much money do you think would be appropriate to pay someone who speaks negatively of others, does not believe in the abilities of her students, is quick to label students and parents as lazy and uncaring, and feels that she should be respected as a professional when she fails to act like one?

The good news is that most teachers do act like professionals. But boy, one bad egg can surely leave a bad taste in your mouth—and might even turn you off to eggs in general. That's why we, as teachers, do not have the luxury of experiencing even one or two unprofessional moments—at least not in public!

True professionals act professionally at all times while they are practicing their chosen professions. Not to say that this is easy. It's not. And sometimes, as professionals, we all need to remind ourselves (or have others remind us) why we chose our profession in the first place. Even the most professional of professionals can benefit from such reminders. Today you'll be reminding everyone of the importance of professionalism in the workplace.

INSERVICE

You might want to begin the inservice by sharing the conversation we just shared with you. Allow the teachers to discuss reasons this teacher was acting in an unprofessional manner. Tell them you realize that teaching is hard work. You realize that it is frustrating. But you do *not* accept the old saying that "teaching is a thankless profession." It's not. Teachers know this the first time a struggling student finally grasps a concept, the first time a student gives them a handmade card thanking them for helping him, the first time a student responds to their tireless efforts by behaving a little better than he usually does, the first time a former student tells them that they made a difference in her life, and on and on. The list is limitless.

Tell your teachers that they are about to engage in an activity that will help them recognize professional and unprofessional behavior. Divide the faculty into two teams. Tell them that the winning team will receive pizza or doughnuts (or whatever) immediately following the game. What you won't tell them is that this game will result in a tie. What you also won't tell them is that this game is simply a means of reminding them that they all need to act professionally at all times. Instead, you're simply playing a game, acting as a great teacher does, making learning fun. The game will take only a few minutes, but its effects will last far longer.

IMPLEMENTATION

Divide the faculty into two teams. Have each team sit together, preferably in a circle. Let each team choose a captain who will answer for the team. The captains will hold a whiteboard or a piece of paper on which they will write the answers for their teams. Tell them you will provide a few sample situations that could take place in a school. Each situation will be accompanied by two options for handling it. The object of the game is to select the more professional of the two options. For each situation, allow time for the captains to consult with their teams and then write their answers. Following each, you will have each captain display her team's answer. One point will be awarded for each correct answer. The team with the most points will win.

We provide a few sample situations here, but we suggest that you make this your own. Fifteen situations will make for a game that lasts less than ten minutes.

Here are a few samples:

1. A teacher doesn't like a new program being implemented schoolwide.

   a. He begins bad-mouthing the program to his coworkers.

   b. He discusses his feelings with the principal, giving reasons he does not like the new program. During this discussion, he offers suggestions as to what he feels would be a more effective program or means of accomplishing whatever this particular program is trying to accomplish.

2. A student is refusing to do work in class.

   a. The teacher talks to the student privately, asking if there is a problem and offering assistance.

   b. The teacher warns the student, in an angry or frustrated tone, that he needs to get busy.

3. Teacher A hears that Teacher B caught her husband cheating on her.

   a. Teacher A tells another teacher of what she has heard about Teacher B.

   b. Teacher A says nothing to anyone.

4. A teacher does not agree with the results of her most recent observation conducted by the principal.

   a. The teacher begins talking to other teachers in order to find out if they are dissatisfied with their observation results. She also discusses her dissatisfaction with her own observation results.

   b. The teacher schedules a meeting with the principal to discuss the reasons for her dissatisfaction. If she is still dissatisfied following the meeting, she schedules a meeting with the next person in the chain of command.

5. A teacher is struggling with classroom management. She cannot seem to get her students to stop talking during class. She cannot seem to get her students to complete assignments.

   a. The teacher enlists the support of a few negative coworkers who she already knows are having trouble with those same students. A griping session about the students ensues.

   b. The teacher seeks advice from a positive teacher who seems to be able to get any student to behave. She asks for a few pointers.

6. A group of teachers is concerned that the dress code policy is not being properly enforced.

   a. The teachers complain about the fact that not everyone is enforcing the policy. They discuss the fact that the administration should do something about this.

   b. The teachers come up with some solutions to the problem and schedule a meeting with the principal to discuss their concerns and offer ideas for a solution.

7. A teacher is confronted by an angry parent. The conference does not go well. The parent leaves, and nothing has been resolved.

   a. The teacher asks a positive coworker or an administrator for suggestions on defusing such a situation in order to deal with this more effectively in the future.

b. The teacher tells everyone who will listen about the conference, sharing her negative opinions of the parent.

Add your own here:

_____

_____

_____

_____

_____

_____

_____

_____

_____

_____

_____

_____

_____

_____

_____

_____

_____

_____

_____

_____

As we discussed earlier, this game will end in a tie, because even though all teachers don't always act professionally, they'll all know the correct answers to the questions. Now you'll have the opportunity to praise your teachers for knowing what professionalism is, to thank them for acting as professionals on a daily basis, and to treat them to refreshments. Also remember that no matter how difficult and frustrating your own job may be, true leaders are always true professionals.

Notes

_____
_____
_____
_____
_____
_____
_____
_____
_____
_____
_____
_____
_____
_____
_____
_____
_____
_____
_____
_____
_____
_____
_____

Shifting Your Focus

PURPOSE

Have you ever bought a car and then suddenly found that everyone seems to have the same car in the same color? You begin seeing that car everywhere. Who opened the factory gates and released all these cars? No gates were opened. These cars were already there. You just never noticed them until your focus shifted.

We've all had days when everything seemed to go wrong. Why is it that when one thing goes wrong, there is often a chain reaction? Often it's because the one thing that went wrong put you into a negative emotional state. While in that state, you began attracting other negative events. Scary, isn't it? The flip side is that when you act from a positive emotional state and choose to focus on what's positive around you, you begin noticing and experiencing more positive events in your life. And yes, this definitely holds true in the classroom.

One of the jobs of a leader is to help keep the people he or she is leading focused on what is positive in the work environment, because that's what increases productivity. Isn't it true that the most positive teachers in your school can find good in almost any student? And isn't it true that the most negative teachers can't seem to find much good in even the most positive and well-behaved students? Again, they truly believe that you give them the "worst kids in the school."

INSERVICE

Begin the inservice with the following activity:

Tell your teachers to look around the room for thirty seconds and try to spot as many objects as they can that are circular or curved. Examples might include a globe, a paperweight, the cap on a beverage bottle, or the face of a clock or watch. Give them thirty seconds to do this and then have them close their eyes. Say, *Keeping your eyes closed, try to remember as many objects as you can that are angular, square, or rectangular.* You will see that at first, most cannot think of even one object. Even those who can think of some are struggling to come up with more than two or three. Now have them open their eyes and look around the room. They will quickly realize that there are many more angles and lines than circles or curves. The desk, the walls, the door, the tiles on the floor, books, boxes, signs—lines are everywhere. Ask them what happened. Why were they struggling to remember even one object with lines or angles?

The answer is, of course, that they were not focusing on those. Mission accomplished. You just helped them prove to themselves that we all tend to "see" only the things on which we focus. In other words, what we focus on becomes our reality. Ask them to relate this to their own lives. Share the example of buying a car. Discuss the familiar experience of the "bad day" chain of events.

When a glass contains liquid that is midway between the top and bottom, is the glass half empty or half full? Allow teachers to answer this and to discuss it as it relates to their lives. Provide a few examples of glass-half-full people versus glass-half-empty people:

1. An accident occurs as you are driving home from work. A glass-half-full person might think, "Wow! That was lucky. Had I left work just a minute

earlier, it could have been me in that accident." A glass-half-empty person might say, "You might know this had to happen right in front of me. Had I left work just a little earlier, I would have been ahead of this accident and this awful traffic."

2. Teachers find out that they are receiving a small raise in pay. A glass-half-full person will be grateful for the extra income. A glass-half-empty person will focus on the fact that it is too little, too late and that the amount of the raise is actually insulting.

3. A principal conducts an inservice where he shares a simple new way to make learning more fun and interesting for the students. A glass-half-full person will take the idea and run with it. A glass-half-empty person will see the new idea as yet more work. (If this example makes a few people in this particular inservice uncomfortable, that's okay. These people just might *need* to feel uncomfortable.)

The third example just provided you with a segue into the next part of the inservice, where teachers will now describe how a glass-half-full teacher might handle situations differently.

1. Two students are off task during one of the lesson's activities. Describe how a glass-half-full teacher might handle this. Describe how a glass-half-empty teacher might handle this. _____

_____

_____

_____

_____

2. A student confides in his teacher that So-and-So is picking on him. What does the glass-half-full teacher do? The glass-half-empty teacher? _____

_____

_____

_____

_____

3. A teacher receives his or her teacher report cards from the students. There are several comments from students mentioning that they don't feel that the teacher allows them enough opportunities to play games and have fun. How does a glass-half-full teacher handle this? A glass-half-empty teacher? _____

_____

_____

_____

_____

Add one or more of your own examples here.

_____

_____

_____

_____

_____

_____

_____

_____

_____

_____

Now ask, *Do you think students would prefer to be in the classroom of a glass-half-empty teacher or a glass-half-full teacher?* Discuss why students respond much more favorably to positive teachers. Your positive teachers will run with this discussion. Your negative teachers, however, are going to feel quite uncomfortable. Again, this is a good thing.

IMPLEMENTATION

Thank the teachers for their participation and responses. Reiterate that what we focus on does tend to become our reality. Be clear: you are not asking them to ignore negative situations that have to be addressed in the classroom. (See Inservice 7, "Learn to Ignore More," for more information on the kinds of behaviors that should and should not be ignored.)

Finally, say, *This week, we will all make an effort to shift our focus. Even the most positive of us can become more positive. By the end of the week, I'd like for everyone to send me a list titled "Twenty-Five Reasons I'm Proud of My Students." Make sure that you get the students' permission to share each item on your list, because these lists are going to go up in the hallway at the end of the week. Thanks, and have fun creating your lists!*

Notes

Inservice 35

The Miracle of Smiling

PURPOSE

Teachers . . . Positive role models . . . People with whom students spend much of their time during their formative years . . . People who are called to a profession that nurtures, molds, and helps promote a hopeful future . . . Motivators, influencers, *life* changers . . . And yet there are people, possibly on your very faculty, who call themselves teachers yet do not look happy.

If you are truly a member of one of the noblest and most influential professions on Earth, shouldn't your actions be noble and your outlook positive? How is it possible to be a motivator and to influence others positively if you are not yourself motivated and positive? Students will always benefit from having happy, positive adults in their lives. Can you name one student who could benefit from having yet another negative influence in his life?

If there are teachers on your faculty who do not appear happy, we suspect that their classrooms are devoid of fun and laughter. And aren't these the very people who have the most student behavior problems? We are not suggesting that a teacher should appear happy when a student does something inappropriate. There are times when it is necessary to appear serious in the classroom. But the times when a teacher should appear unhappy are few and far between. Overall, effective teachers appear happy. Whether they're as happy on the inside as they appear on the outside is irrelevant, because the students can't tell the difference.

Do you agree that if you could get all your teachers to appear even a little happier, there would be an instant difference in your overall school climate? Would you believe that some teachers actually think that if they appear serious, they will maintain better control of their students? These are the teachers who warn the new teachers not to smile until Christmas!

Because teachers are human, and because teaching can be a difficult job at times, many teachers fall into the habit of appearing way too serious way too often. Sometimes they just need a reminder. You, their leader, can offer this reminder.

INSERVICE

Begin today's inservice by asking, *How many of you believe that students need more positive role models in their lives?* Your teachers will readily agree that all students could benefit from more positive role models. None of us can ever have enough positive role models in our lives. Next, ask, *At school, who are the adult role models in our students' lives?* They will answer that they are. Now for the zinger. Ask, *Would you believe me if I told you that there are teachers (though, we hope, not in our school) who do not appear happy?* You'll get a laugh from the majority of your teachers. But guess who won't find the humor in that thought? Your negative teachers. Ask, *Can any of you name even one student who could benefit from having yet another negative influence in his life?* They won't be able to name a student, because no such student exists. Tell them that students need and deserve to have happy adults in their lives. And although we cannot control what goes on in their home lives, we can absolutely control what goes on at school.

At this point, no matter how silly you will appear, simply look at your teachers and smile at them. Don't say anything. Just keep smiling. We assure you that the majority of them will smile back. Ask them what just happened, and let them figure it out and discuss it briefly.

Next, share with your teachers a few of the benefits of smiling:

- When you smile, even if your smile is feigned, your brain releases stress fighters called endorphins. These are our natural painkillers. This release of endorphins makes us feel happier. Again, even if the smile is not genuine, the endorphins still get released. You become happier even if you don't want to!

- Smiles are contagious. (You just proved that point when you smiled at them.)

- It is almost impossible for a student to misbehave when you are smiling at him. If you don't believe this, try it.

- Students respond more favorably to positive teachers than they do to negative teachers.

- Because we want our students to respond favorably to us, one of the easiest ways to accomplish this is to smile more often.

- Smiling at someone sends a message that you care about her. When a student believes that you care, she is much more likely to learn from you and to behave well in your presence.

- Smiles are free, but their results are priceless.

IMPLEMENTATION

Tell your teachers that there is simply no downside to smiling more often. Say, *Let's try a one-week experiment. Let's all make an extra effort to smile more than we normally do in our classrooms. I'll be participating also by smiling more at students when I encounter them in the hallways or when I visit your classrooms. When I do come into your classrooms this week, I'll only be looking for one thing: your pearly whites!* Make it clear that you are not asking any of them to actually *be* happy. You're simply asking them to *appear* happy.

You'll see the results immediately. Comment all week long on the smiles you are witnessing. Then bring them back together at the end of the week. Share your observations and ask them to share their own. We have helped many principals conduct this experiment, and the results are never short of amazing. Recently, several teachers admitted to us that their students asked them if something was wrong because they seemed too happy! We all got a laugh out of that, but these teachers received an important message from their students. Students want and deserve happy adults in their lives. Help your teachers be those adults.

Notes

_____
_____
_____
_____
_____
_____
_____
_____
_____
_____
_____
_____
_____
_____
_____
_____
_____
_____
_____
_____
_____
_____
_____

Are You All Right?

PURPOSE

FACT: Students' attitudes and demeanors in a classroom often mirror those of the teacher.

FACT: Students who believe that their teacher cares about them are more likely to behave appropriately than students who do not believe that the teacher cares about them.

FACT: Inappropriate questions can provoke inappropriate responses.

FACT: Dealing privately with student misbehavior removes the "audience" and increases the chances that the conference will be productive.

Have you ever heard an angry teacher ask a student, "What's the matter with you?" Another popular question is a snide, "Do you have a problem?" You do realize, of course, that both of these are rhetorical. The teacher is not truly expressing concern and indicating that she is willing to offer some support. Students definitely realize this, and they usually respond to these types of "questions" with defiance. Inadvertently, the teacher is setting students up to retaliate with an attitude that mirrors her own. This is never productive and is always unprofessional. There are much more appropriate and productive ways of finding out what's bothering a student or what's causing him to misbehave. Today you'll be sharing one simple technique for dealing effectively with a student who is doing something inappropriate.

INSERVICE

Demonstrate for your teachers the rhetorical questions we just shared with you. Ask if they've ever heard or said the following:

- What's the matter with you? (in an angry tone)

- Do you have a problem? (in an angry tone)

Now ask,

- Is the teacher who is asking those questions expressing caring and concern or frustration?

- How would most students respond to those questions?

- Would you agree that the teacher, probably without realizing it, has just laid the groundwork for a power struggle?

- Is there anything positive that can come from power struggles?

Tell your teachers that today you will be sharing a simple technique for dealing with inappropriate student behavior.

The technique is called the "Are You All Right?" technique. It is based on the simple premise that students who believe you care about them are much more apt to behave better. Here's what you do. The next time a student misbehaves, take him aside (not in front of his peers) and ask, "Are you all right?" (You ask this, of course, with a voice and demeanor of caring and concern.) You might be surprised at the look on the student's face. Almost always, the student will answer, "Yes." Then say, "Well, the reason I was asking is that the way you were behaving in class was inappropriate and not at all like you." (Okay, so maybe you're stretching the truth a little, as the behavior is perhaps very typical of that student.) Continue by saying, "I knew that for you to be acting that way, something must be bothering you. And I just want you to know that I'm here for you if you'd like to talk about it."

That's it! It takes only a few seconds. Did you deal with the misbehavior? Yes. You made it clear that it was inappropriate. Will the student's behavior improve? Almost always!

Please note that what you did not *do was very important. You did not dare him to do it again. You did not act personally offended by his actions. You did not threaten him. You did not belittle him. You simply expressed caring and concern.*

IMPLEMENTATION

As you send your teachers off to attempt this technique, remind them of the following:

- The "Are You All Right?" technique is a nonthreatening, respectful way to deal with a student's inappropriate behavior.

- Remember to display only a demeanor of caring and concern when using this technique. It will not work if you appear flustered or sarcastic.

- Remember that if a student feels that you genuinely care about him as a person, he is much more likely to behave better and to work harder in your classroom.

- The technique usually takes less than a minute to implement. It's quick, it's free, it takes no extra planning on your part, it promotes a better relationship between teachers and students, and it works beautifully. *Try it.*

The italicized section is from Annette Breaux and Todd Whitaker, *Making Good Teaching Great* (Larchmont, NY: Eye on Education, 2012), p. 98. www.eyeoneducation.com

Notes

Your Favorite Teacher

PURPOSE

If you take any group of teachers and ask how many of them were positively influenced by a teacher in their young lives, almost every hand will go up. In fact, many of the world's greatest teachers chose the teaching profession in response to the influence of teachers in their own lives. Next to parents, teachers may be the most influential people on Earth! Consider the fact that between the ages of five and eighteen, many students spend more waking hours with their teachers than they do with their parents! Along with profound influence comes tremendous responsibility. And one of the best ways to remind teachers of the power of their influence is to have them remember their favorite teacher.

INSERVICE

Begin the inservice by telling a story about your own favorite teacher. Who was that person? What kinds of qualities did he or she possess? Why was that teacher your favorite? How did that teacher treat you? How did that teacher make you feel about yourself?

Next, have all close their eyes and think about their all-time favorite teacher. Then have the teachers think of five special qualities of their favorite teacher. Have a volunteer write teachers' responses on the board or on chart paper (large enough for all to see). You may or may not be surprised to learn that their list will look very similar to this one:

- My favorite teacher cared about me.
- My favorite teacher was very positive, always smiling.
- My favorite teacher loved teaching.
- My favorite teacher made learning fun.
- My favorite teacher never yelled at us.
- My favorite teacher believed in me.
- My favorite teacher never embarrassed me.
- My favorite teacher made me feel special.
- My favorite teacher made me feel successful.

You might also be surprised to see that no one ever mentions the number of degrees their favorite teacher possessed or the wonderful textbooks from which their favorite teacher taught. The qualities teachers recall tend to focus on how their favorite teacher made them *feel*—successful, loved, special, capable, and so on. Point this out after they come up with their list.

Next, and possibly most important, discuss what was *not* mentioned on the list. The following characteristics are never included when teachers remember their favorite teacher:

- My favorite teacher was mean to me.

- My favorite teacher was so negative.

- My favorite teacher gave really difficult tests.

- My favorite teacher had a really high IQ.

- My favorite teacher yelled at me a lot.

We could go on, but the list is starting to look like the list in Inservice 38, during which teachers will remember their least favorite teacher.

Next, pointing to the list of characteristics of your teachers' favorite teachers, ask, *Are these the same characteristics your students would list about you?* Don't be surprised if you hear a little laughter. Sometimes people use humor to cover their insecurities. You may notice that the people laughing will be the ones whose relationships with students leave much to be desired. Then ask, *Would your students list you as their favorite teacher? If not, why not?* (These are rhetorical questions. You just want your teachers to pause and think.)

IMPLEMENTATION

Have your teachers copy at least ten items from the group's list. We don't suggest giving them a copy, as writing their own list may help cement the importance of the characteristics of favorite teachers.

Say to your teachers, *Even if you don't possess all of these characteristics today, you can begin possessing them tomorrow. Every child deserves the kind of teacher you discussed today.* Be *that teacher.*

Notes

_____
_____
_____
_____
_____
_____
_____
_____
_____
_____
_____
_____
_____
_____
_____
_____
_____
_____
_____
_____
_____
_____
_____
_____
_____
_____
_____
_____
_____
_____

Your Least Favorite Teacher

PURPOSE

We often remind teachers that they live inside the hearts and minds of every student they have ever taught. A teacher's influence on a student, positive or negative, has nothing to do with that student's good or bad behavior. Rather it has everything to do with that *teacher's* good or bad behavior.

All students deserve to have every teacher serve as a positive influence in their young lives. They deserve to have teachers who care about them, who will not give up on them, and who will help them realize their potential. They deserve nothing but our very best. Reality tells us, however, that this is not always what they receive.

Sadly, negative influences can be every bit as lasting as positive ones. One of the best ways to remind teachers of how lasting a negative influence can be is to remind them of their least favorite teachers.

INSERVICE

Begin the inservice by telling the story of your least favorite teacher (no names, please). What qualities did *that* person possess? Why was that teacher your least favorite? How did that teacher treat you? How did that teacher make you feel about yourself?

Next, have everyone close his eyes and think about his all-time least favorite teacher. Don't be surprised if you hear a collective sigh. Ask each teacher to think of five qualities of his least favorite teacher. Have a volunteer write teachers' responses on the board or on chart paper (large enough for all to see). You may or may not be surprised to learn that their list will look very similar to this one:

- My least favorite teacher was so negative. (You'll also hear "bitter," "angry," "cynical," and "mean.")
- My least favorite teacher seemed to dislike teaching.
- My least favorite teacher seemed to dislike students.
- My least favorite teacher's class was boring.
- My least favorite teacher yelled a lot.
- My least favorite teacher never smiled.
- My least favorite teacher was intimidating.
- My least favorite teacher did not believe in me.
- My least favorite teacher often embarrassed or humiliated students.

This list will be the polar opposite of the list from the previous inservice, during which your teachers listed qualities of their favorite teacher. Notice that some of your teachers still feel very negatively about their least favorite teacher. Notice and point out that your teachers still remember, quite vividly, their least favorite teacher. Although we might all like to forget this person, it's next to impossible to do so. That's because this person left a lasting impression on us. Negative, but lasting.

Next, pointing to the list of characteristics of your teachers' least favorite teachers, ask, *Would any of your students say any of these things about you?* Again, don't be surprised if you hear a little laughter. Then ask, rhetorically, of course, *Would any of your students mention you as their least favorite teacher? If so, why?*

At this point, you'll want to quickly add, *I'm sure that none of you possess any of these characteristics, but it's a good idea to keep in mind the qualities that you do not ever want to possess. It has often been said that even on your worst day, you're some student's best hope. Our students are counting on us. They all need and deserve a place to come to each day that is teeming with nothing but positive people who serve as positive role models in their lives. Remember that we are role models. We are professionals. None of us want to be remembered in a negative way by any of our students. And we certainly don't want to have a negative influence on any student's life.*

IMPLEMENTATION

Have your teachers copy at least ten items from the group's list. Say to them, *Even if you don't possess any of these characteristics we've listed today, it's a good idea to keep this list handy as a reminder of what you never want to become. No child, regardless of his behavior, deserves the kinds of teachers you discussed today. Don't ever allow yourselves to become, in any way, like those teachers.*

Notes

_____

_____

_____

_____

_____

_____

_____

_____

_____

_____

_____

_____

_____

The Psychology of an Apology

PURPOSE

The best way to get in the last word is to apologize.

Have you ever had one of those "Wow, I wish I hadn't said that" moments? A moment when you realized that you had said something, whether intentionally or inadvertently, that hurt someone else's feelings? Teachers work with a great variety of students (and adults) in a sometimes stressful, always demanding occupation. Over the course of a school year, there are times when they do not always respond to students, parents, or co-workers appropriately. To err is human . . .

Most teachers work very hard at establishing and maintaining positive relationships with their students. They realize that before you can teach a student, you have to reach a student. Students truly don't care how much we know until they know how much we care. However, as superhuman as teachers attempt to be, there are times when even the very best teachers are not always *at* their very best. They say or do things that hurt or humiliate a student, usually without realizing it.

There's good news and bad news. The bad news first: when a teacher says or does something to hurt a student's feelings, the relationship between the teacher and the student is immediately damaged. When the relationship is damaged, the student will be less likely to do his best or behave his best in this teacher's classroom. Thus, not only have the student's feelings been hurt, but his learning and behavior may suffer also. His image of the teacher has changed. Respect has been lost, trust has been lost, and he may even view the teacher as a threat. None of this is conducive to learning. But here's the good news: students are so very forgiving. Any teacher who has ever apologized to a student can attest to the fact that if you apologize to a student, he will almost always say two words, "That's okay." And he will forgive you. The simple act of apologizing can repair damage, reestablish trust, and lead to newfound respect. Also, when a teacher apologizes for a hurtful act, he is serving as a good role model for what anyone should do when he says or does something hurtful. We can hope that students will learn, from the teacher's example, to follow suit when they say or do hurtful things to others.

As a leader, you must continually work to help build and refine the skills of every teacher in your school. Adding to each teacher's tool kit is essential. Your best teachers usually have no trouble apologizing when they have done something to hurt someone, be it a child or an adult. Your less than best teachers, however, often get caught up in defending their actions, and they actually work very hard to convince themselves and everyone else that their actions were justified. Regardless of the effectiveness or ineffectiveness of the teacher who hurts a student's feelings, the student's feelings are still hurt, and the relationship needs to be repaired. Today you will be sharing one simple way of apologizing that maintains the dignity of both the apologizer and the person offended and that helps repair any damage caused by a hurtful act.

INSERVICE

Share an experience where you have said or done something that you regretted, either immediately or upon reflection. Also describe a situation where someone did something to you that still stings, even though it may have happened long ago.

Now ask the group, *How many of you have experienced situations where you were not quite as patient with a student as you wish you had been?* One or two teachers may wish to share their experiences. Say, *It may have been as simple as rolling your eyes or as harsh as a cutting remark, but most of us have at some point hurt a student's feelings. Once we do, we may instantly regret our actions, or it may take a while for us to realize what we've done. Sometimes, stubborn pride can prevent us from backing down, because we firmly believe the student caused the situation.*

Next, ask, *What alternatives are there? What if you know a student's feelings have been hurt, but you're not quite sure that you were wrong? Sometimes it's as simple as saying, "I am sorry that happened."* Before you go any further, make it clear that saying, "I was wrong, I'm sorry, and I hope you can forgive me" is the way to apologize when the teacher knows he was wrong. But if he's not quite sure that he was wrong, saying "I am sorry that happened" can help heal the damaged relationship between the teacher and the student. He's not saying that he was wrong, technically speaking. But he is saying that he's truly sorry the situation happened. At this point, you might wish to discuss the good news–bad news paragraph in the Purpose section of this inservice. You want to cement the point that maintaining positive relationships with students is vital.

Now ask the group, *Have any of you ever had a student cheat on a quiz or a test? Almost all of us have. An easy way to maintain a positive relationship with the student, regardless of his actions, is to say, "I am sorry that happened." This does not mean that there will not be consequences. However, it does allow us to keep the relationship intact. When a student arrives late to class and offers yet another excuse, you can say, "I am sorry that happened." Again, this does not mean that there will not be consequences.*

Yet another time to use the phrase "I am sorry that happened" is when you receive a phone call from an irate parent. Saying something like, "I am sorry that happened" can help defuse the parent and de-escalate the tone of the conversation. You might be thinking that you didn't do anything wrong. You might be correct. However, anytime we have to deal with an angry parent, isn't it true that we are always sorry it happened, whatever the "it" was?

IMPLEMENTATION

Ask the teachers to share, in pairs, situations where saying "I am sorry that happened" would have been a more effective way to deal with the situation than the way they chose to deal with it. Ask them to begin practicing using the "I am sorry that happened" phrase when a student shares that he forgot his homework or could not get his locker open or fell down at recess and skinned his knee. By using this phrase on a regular basis when they are not feeling intense stress, they will be more likely to use it when they are. The technique is simple and highly effective. Using it can temper a negative situation or defuse a person's emotions almost instantly while maintaining dignity and protecting relationships.

Notes

_____
_____
_____
_____
_____
_____
_____
_____
_____
_____
_____
_____
_____
_____
_____
_____
_____
_____
_____

A Teacher's Creed

PURPOSE

If you were to ask students—any students of any age level in any school—to describe their ideal teacher, can't you already predict what they would say? Don't you know, without even asking, what students want, need, and deserve from their teachers? If you were to give students statements to complete beginning with "The ideal teacher would _____" and "The ideal teacher would not _____," you might be surprised to learn how similar everyone's answers would be. Although no two students' answers would be identical, the characteristics they would name would likely include the following:

- The ideal teacher would be nice. (*Note:* You'll see this one almost every time.)

- The ideal teacher would make learning fun.

- The ideal teacher would be helpful.

- The ideal teacher would not embarrass me.
- The ideal teacher would not make me feel bad about myself.
- The ideal teacher would not yell at me.
- The ideal teacher would not compare me to other students.
- The ideal teacher would smile a lot.
- The ideal teacher would listen to me.
- The ideal teacher would not have favorites.
- The ideal teacher would treat us fairly.
- The ideal teacher would challenge me.
- The ideal teacher would explain new concepts so that I could understand.
- The ideal teacher would love teaching.
- The ideal teacher would care about me as a person.
- The ideal teacher would not give too much homework.
- The ideal teacher would let us play games.
- The ideal teacher would forgive me if I did something wrong.
- The ideal teacher would have rules, but not too many.
- The ideal teacher would be encouraging.

Can you think of one item on this list that is unreasonable? We can't. Students want to learn and succeed. And they want to learn and succeed in the classrooms of caring teachers. That's the least we should be able to guarantee them. Every student, every year, every classroom.

Take another look at the list. It probably describes some of your teachers perfectly. But don't others fall short? Today you'll help them all become more aware of what students want, need, and deserve. You'll encourage them all to strive toward becoming that ideal teacher.

INSERVICE

Ask your teachers, *If you were to ask students, any students, to describe their ideal teacher and give statements beginning with "The ideal teacher would _____" and "The ideal teacher would not _____," do you think you could predict some of their answers?* At this point, several teachers might laugh about the fact that some students would say things like "The ideal teacher would let us stay home" or "The ideal teacher would not give us any work to do." Yes, occasionally teachers might receive these types of responses. Remind them, however, that if you gave them such statements to complete about the ideal principal, a few of them might be tempted to answer similarly!

Allow the teachers a few minutes to predict, as a group, what students might say. (Write some of their answers here in order to compare them to the list we provided. You might also choose to have someone write the group's answers on the board or on chart paper.)

The ideal teacher would _____.

The ideal teacher would not _____.

The ideal teacher would _____.

The ideal teacher would not _____.

The ideal teacher would _____.

The ideal teacher would not _____.

The ideal teacher would _____.

The ideal teacher would not _____.

The ideal teacher would _____.

The ideal teacher would not _____.

After the discussion, share and compare both lists. Ask if they feel that any of these statements are unreasonable. Discuss that it's not always easy being the kind of teacher students need you to be. Teaching effectively is not easy. But it *is* rewarding.

IMPLEMENTATION

Combine the lists and turn them into a Teacher's Creed. Encourage *all* your teachers to display this creed in their classrooms and, more important, to be the kind of teachers their students deserve.

The following is a sample Teacher's Creed. Feel free to use ours or to help your teachers create their own.

> ### *My Promises to You, My Students:*
>
> *I promise to be nice and smile often.*
> *I promise to care about each of you.*
> *I promise to be understanding.*
> *I promise to help you when you are struggling.*
> *I promise to be patient with you.*
> *I promise to be fair and consistent.*
> *I promise to enjoy teaching you.*
> *I promise to be trustworthy.*
> *I promise never to scream at you.*
> *I promise that I will get to know you.*
> *I promise to believe in you.*
> *I promise to make learning interesting and meaningful.*
> *I promise that I will not intentionally embarrass you.*
> *I promise that I will challenge you to be your very best.*
> *I promise to do everything I can to help you succeed.*
> *And I promise that, no matter what, I will never give up on you.*
>
> "My Promises to You, My Students" is from Annette Breaux and Todd Whitaker,
> *Seven Simple Secrets: What the BEST Teachers Know and Do* (Larchmont, NY:
> Eye on Education, 2006), p. 105. www.eyeoneducation.com

Imagine what your school would be like if *all* your teachers offered and kept these promises! Help them do just that.

Notes

Appendix

Tips for Effective Presentations

The following material is designed to assist you, the administrator or staff developer, in maximizing the effectiveness of each inservice. It will also

- Provide additional tips for making any presentation successful
- Help you personalize the inservices provided in the book
- Help you hone your presentation skills

TEN SECRETS OF SUCCESSFUL PRESENTATIONS

1. **Be enthusiastic**. *Your* enthusiasm can make or break a presentation. If you've ever attended an inservice led by a less than enthusiastic presenter, you know this to be true. Regardless of the content and the speaker's knowledge, a lackluster presenter will lose his audience every time. After all, if the speaker doesn't seem to buy what he's selling, why should the audience?

2. **Share personal stories**. One of your main jobs as a presenter is to connect with your audience. And there's no better way to do that than to share a few personal anecdotes. People will remember a personal story much more readily than they will remember research or data.

For instance, if you're teaching teachers the importance of maintaining their composure with their students, you might wish to share a story about a time when you failed to maintain your composure. Talk about what happened before, during, and after you lost your cool. Tell what you wish you would have done differently. By doing this, you now have your audience thinking, "Hey, she's a real person who has made real mistakes and has learned real lessons. I can relate to that!"

3. **Prepare!** No matter how long you have been presenting, you cannot "wing it"—not successfully, anyway. Audiences can always tell whether a presenter is or is not prepared. Although you don't want to read from a script, you do want to have an outline that is well prepared and that will keep you on point with your message. Practice your presentation beforehand. In this case, the mirror is your friend. Practice delivering your content, practice varying your tone of voice when you make specific points, and practice using positive body language! You want to come across as well prepared, approachable, believable, positive, passionate, and confident.

4. **Make it relevant**. People have no interest in learning about things that they don't feel hold personal meaning or relevance. In order for your audience to realize the importance of your message, they must feel that your message is relevant to them, today! Don't assume that they will automatically make the connection and see the relevance in your message. Spell it out for them. Tell them exactly how they can use the information or skills in their lives.

5. **Make eye contact!** Effective presenters speak directly to the audience, deliberately attempting to make eye contact with each attendee. This helps each person feel as though the speaker is speaking directly to him or her, cementing that oh-so-important personal connection between "teacher" and "student."

6. **Laugh!** Effective presenters know the importance of injecting humor into their presentations. They want the audience to enjoy the presentation and to feel at ease. An occasional funny story or corny joke can help accomplish this.

7. **Involve your audience**. Be careful not to talk "at" your audience. From start to finish, you want audience participation. That participation can take many forms—discussions, questions, activities, and so on. An engaged audience is much more likely to absorb the ideas and information you are sharing.

8. **Walk your talk**. Audiences want to feel as though a presenter can relate to them, is sympathetic to their situations, and has "been there and done that." If you're addressing a group of teachers and discussing the importance of laughing with their students, yet you appear serious and are not laughing with your audience, you won't get much buy-in. If your actions are incongruent with your words, your actions will win every time. So model the behavior you want to see in your audience.

9. **Make the lessons you teach simple and doable**. When you present information in a way that seems simple and doable, the audience is more apt to listen intently, consider the

information you are sharing, and attempt to implement the new ideas, tips, and strategies you have shared in your presentation. If, in contrast, something you share seems difficult or time-consuming, your audience will quickly go into "overwhelm mode" and disconnect. So teach in small bites, just as effective teachers do in the classroom. You want your audience leaving you thinking, "I can do this!"

10. **Ask for feedback and *use* that feedback**. Let your audience know that what they think *matters*! Address all their comments with thoughtfulness and appreciation, even in the event that a comment is disagreeable.

FREQUENTLY ASKED QUESTIONS

How do I personalize the inservices?

These inservices are not set in stone. Please feel free to add your own personal touch to each. The key is to make each inservice suit the needs of your audience. Supplement any inservice with personal stories, your own experiences, and your own ideas.

How do I use these inservices to change the way my teachers teach?

These inservices have been designed to be short and quick, yet highly effective. Just as students learn best and experience more success when we teach in small bites, the same holds true for teachers. Conduct one inservice in ten minutes and send the teachers off to implement and practice what they have learned. Praise their efforts on the days following the inservice, and lend a hand when a teacher is struggling. Nothing about any of the inservices should be overwhelming, time-consuming, or difficult. By the end of the week, one simple ten-minute inservice will have had an impact on the effectiveness of your teachers, the climate of your school, or both. Lather, rinse, repeat!

Do each of the inservices have to last only ten minutes?

Quite simply, no. These inservices do not have to last only ten minutes. You are the leader, and it is up to you to decide how and when you would like to use these inservices and how long or brief you would like for each to be. For instance, let's say that you are implementing a particular inservice and the discussion becomes more involved than you had anticipated. If, for some reason, you decide you'd like to go ahead and run with this discussion and allow it to continue beyond the suggested two or three minutes, then do so. Or you might decide to carry it over into your next meeting. That's fine. Again, it's your call. Another example would be if you send your teachers off to implement a new strategy and realize that they need more training in that particular strategy. By all means, provide that training. Although each inservice is designed to last ten minutes, it does not mean that each *has* to last only ten minutes.

Does the principal or staff developer have to conduct all the inservices?

No. Assistant administrators, star teachers, or anyone you deem qualified can conduct some of the inservices. For example, Inservice 20 is titled "Twenty-Five Reasons to Be Proud of Our School." A principal might have one or two of her star teachers conduct this particular inservice, during which the entire faculty will come up with a list of twenty-five reasons they are proud of the school.

FIVE THINGS TO REMEMBER WHEN USING THIS BOOK

1. Your own buy-in as an administrator or staff developer will make or break the success of these inservices. Just as students have to believe that their teacher believes in what he or she is teaching and is actually happy to be teaching it, the same holds true for anyone presenting information to a group of teachers. If you appear in any way lackluster or less than enthusiastic, the teachers will never buy in to what you are teaching them. If you approach an inservice as though you are simply the "messenger," the inservice will not be successful. Just as teachers are role models for their students, you are a role model for your teachers. Quite simply, if you don't buy in to what you're saying, neither will they.

2. Use the Notes section to write about what works well for each inservice and what doesn't. If you have ideas as to how to better implement an inservice, include them in your notes so that next year, that particular inservice will be that much more effective.

3. Don't make the inservices seem like a chore. You want each to be something your teachers look forward to with excitement. So your buildup to each will be key. Publicize each upcoming ten-minute inservice—treat it as a big event, something to look forward to!

4. Follow-through is vital to the success of any inservice training session. It's easy to walk away from a great inservice feeling motivated and energized. What's difficult is to maintain that level of energy once you leave the inservice and reenter reality. That is why follow-through is critical. After you've conducted an inservice for teachers and sent them to go forth and implement, follow through by observing the implementation or communicating with your teachers regarding their successes and struggles with the new strategies they have learned. Praise every effort you observe and provide ongoing encouragement.

5. If you're delegating the responsibility for conducting one or more of the inservices to someone else, make sure that that "someone else" is competent, capable, and credible.

Index

D

Decision making, student-based, 147–150

Delegating responsibilities, 195

Desks, teachers', 61, 62

Displays, classroom, 107, 108

E

Early finishers, 52, 54

Effective teaching: enthusiasm and, 56–58; fun activities in, 72–75; importance of, 48; versus ineffective teaching, 44–45; meaningful lessons in, 68–71; recognizing, 43; report cards for, 121–128; strategies for increasing, 45, 48–49; student engagement and, 51–54; student-based decisions in, 147–150; teachers' creed and, 185–188; teachers' movement around room and, 65–66; teachers' observation of, 139–142; using inservice to promote, 193–194

Emotional control, lack of, 23–30, 36–40

Enabling negative teachers, 103, 104

Endorphins, 168

Engagement, of students, 51–52

Enthusiasm: during Back to School Night, 80, 82; of principals, 70, 83, 84, 191; of teachers, 56–58, 85

Eye contact, 192

F

Faculty meetings: goal of, 1; greeting teachers at, 84; length of, 1; seating arrangement during, 64, 65; securing audience attention at, 8

Favorite teachers, 174–180

Feedback: for principals, from teachers, 130–133, 193; for teachers, from students, 121–128

Follow-through, 87–88, 195

Football games, 60

Fun lessons, 72–74

G

Gossip, 104, 111–112

Greeting students, 83–85

Gripe sessions, 134, 135

H

Habits, 64–65

Humor, 192

I

Ignoring misbehavior, 31–35

Inservices: benefits of, 2; capturing audience attention during, 6; effective presentations in, 191–195; follow-through with, 87–88, 195; goal of, 47; greeting teachers at, 84; leaders of, 194; length of, 1, 194; review meeting for, 87–89

Invitations, for Back to School Night, 80–82

Isolation, of teachers, 134–135

L

Last word, 181

Laughter, 192

Learning, incorporating fun into, 72–75

Lecturing, 72

Lesson planning: for bell-to-bell teaching, 52, 54; coaches versus teachers and, 60, 61, 62; fun activities in, 72–75; meaningful activities in, 68–71; sharing ideas for, 74

Likeable teachers, 152–154

M

Meaningful lessons, 68–71

Meetings. *See* Faculty meetings

Misbehavior: audience for, 15; consequences and, 13; contacting parents about, 117; effective versus ineffective strategies for, 48–49; ignoring of, 31–35; negative co-workers and, 103; questioning students about, 170–172; screaming at students for,

23–26; smiling and, 168; strategies for managing, 16–18; teachers' loss of emotional control due to, 23–30; teachers' mistakes related to, 15, 16; teachers' movement around room and, 65–66

Motivation, of students: coaches versus teachers and, 59, 61, 62; likeable teachers and, 152–154

N

Negativity: of co-workers, 101–104; focusing on, 91–92, 161–165; of least favorite teachers, 178–180; on principal report cards, 132–133; professionalism and, 155–156; teacher collaboration and, 134, 135; teachers' lounge and, 110, 111, 112

No Screaming policy, 25

Notes, to parents, 115–116

O

Off-task behavior, 66

Organized workspaces, 106–109

P

Parents: defusing anger from, 36–40; involvement of, 79–82, 115; positive communication with, 114–118

Personal stories, 192

Personalized inservice, 193

Phone calls to parents: for Back to School Night, 80; positive notes home and, 117

Popularity, of teachers, 152, 153

Positive school environment, 92–95; focusing on, 161–165; smiling and, 166–169; teachers' lounge and, 110–111, 112

Power struggles, 31, 38

Practice, 60, 62

Presentations, 191–195

Pride, in school, 91–95

Principals: effective presentations of, 191–195; enthusiasm of, 70, 191; goal of, 2; inservice organization and, xii; positive focus of, 162; report cards for, 130–133

Private practice session technique, 16–18

Prizes: for Back to School Night, 81, 82; for welcoming classroom environments, 109

Procedures: consequences for violating, 13; establishment of, 10–13; versus rules, 12; for securing student attention, 7–8

Professionalism: characteristics of, 156–159; defusing anger and, 39; negativity and, 155–156; screaming and, 24, 25, 28

Q

Questioning students, about misbehavior, 170–172

R

Recess, 16–18

Relationship building: apologies and, 181–182; likeable teachers and, 152–154; positive notes and, 117–118; questioning students and, 171–172; teachers' creed and, 185–188

Relevance, 192

Reminder inservice, 87–89

Report cards: for principals, 130–133; for teachers, 121–128

Respect, 182

Rhetorical questions, 170–172

Role models: principals as, 194–195; smiling of, 167–168; teachers as, 24–25

Rules, classroom: common mistake regarding, 11; establishment of, 10–13; versus procedures, 12

S

School climate: classroom environment and, 106–109; greeting students and, 83–84; negative co-workers and, 101–104; parent communication and, 114–118; parent involvement and, 79–82; reminder inservice and, 87–89; school pride and, 91–95; student appreciation and, 96–99; teachers' lounge and, 110–113

School pride, 91–95

Screaming at students, 23–26, 27–28

Seating arrangements, 64–65

Serious appearance, 167

Sharing sessions, 134–138

Signals, for securing student attention, 7

Skill practice, 61, 62

Smiling, 84, 111, 166–168

Staff developers, 2

Storytelling, 192

Stress, 168

Struggling teachers: bell-to-bell teaching by, 54; sharing classroom management strategies with, 19–22

Student achievement: benefits of inservice for, 2; celebrating, 57; effective teaching and, 48; fun activities for, 72–75; meaningful lessons and, 68

Student Appreciation Week, 96–99

Student-based decisions, 147–150

Students: apologizing to, 181–184; appreciation for, 96–99; celebrating success of, 57, 96; daily greeting of, 83–85; defusing anger from, 36–40; displaying work of, 107, 108; as early finishers of class activities, 52; teacher report cards from, 121–128

Sympathetic leaders, 193

T

Talking in class: rule against, 11, 12, 13; strategy for addressing, 16–18

Teachers: acknowledging progress of, 89; as actors, 56, 57, 58; characteristics of effective, 175, 185–186; as coaches, 59–63; collaboration of, 134–138; enthusiasm of, 56–58; favorite versus least favorite, 174–180; human nature of, 181–182; influence of, 174–175; isolation of, 134–135; location of, in classroom, 61, 62, 64–66; loss of control by, 23–26; movement of, around classroom, 65–66; negative attitude of, 101–104; observations of teachers by, 139–142; organized workspaces of, 106–109; popularity of, 152, 153; report cards for, 121–128; as role models, 24–25; sharing of strategies by, 19–22; types of, 2

Teachers' creed, 185–188

Teachers' lounge, 110–113

Teaching, effective. See Effective teaching

Time fillers, 54

Trust, establishing, 182

W

Walmart, 84

Welcoming environment, 107, 108

Whitaker, T., 188, 197

A Final Word

Anyone who helps a teacher become more effective has a positive impact on every student whom the teacher will teach from today forward. If as an administrator, mentor, or staff developer you have used this book to help even one teacher improve only a little, you've made a significant difference. If you have used these inservices to benefit your entire faculty, the results could be profound.

We hope that you have found these inservices to be practical, useful, and easy to implement. We also hope that as a result of the inservices, you have witnessed improvements in your faculty's teaching skills and attitudes, in student achievement, and in your school's climate.

We encourage you to continue using the inservices year after year. No school can be too effective, and no teachers can ever become too good at reaching and teaching students. All students deserve our very best. Thank you for giving them yours!

CONTACT US!

We'd love to hear from you about how you are using the inservices and how they are affecting your teachers, your students, and your school. If you have questions, we'd love to have the chance to try to answer them. We really do like to hear from our readers, as our readers' comments help us write better books. So don't be shy: email us!

Todd Whitaker: Todd.Whitaker@indstate.edu

Annette Breaux: AnnetteLBreaux@yahoo.com

All poetry in this book is the original work of Annette Breaux.